COUNTRY BASKET

To Mau and Filippo, remembering that November day spent cutting branches in the rain

ACKNOWLEDGEMENTS

Maurizio Minora, Giorgio Carenzi, Bernadetta Pazzielli, Mariarita Macchiavelli, Giuseppe Jacona, Chiara and Amedeo, Barbara, Marina, Angelo and Mariapia, Anna, Lucio, Donatella and Ezio, my mother and sister.
Germano Melotti and the Doro di Monno (Brescia, Italy).
Donatella Sini of the Cooperativa "Il Cigno" of Castelsardo (Sassari, Italy)
The Weaving Museum in Castelsardo
The Tiranese Ethnographic Museum (Sondrio, Italy)
The firms which supplied some of the material photographed:
Habitat – Studio Alam, Via Bramante 9, Milan.
La Porcellana Bianca, Via Statuto 11, Milan.
IKEA, Via Marchesi 4, Corsico, Milan.
Penelopi 3, Piazza San Marco 1, Milan.
Koivu, Corso Europa 12, Milan.

My special thanks to the photographers Alberto and Mario.

Editor: Cristina Sperandeo
Photography: Alberto Bertoldi and Mario Matteucci
Graphic design and layout: Paola Masera and Amelia Verga with Beatrice Brancaccio
Translation: Chiara Tarsia

Library of Congress Cataloging-in-Publication Data Available
10 9 8 7 6 5 4 3 2 1

Published by Sterling Publishing Company, Inc.
387 Park Avenue South, New York, N.Y. 10016
First published in Italy by R.C.S. Libri S.p.A.
under the title *Cesteria*
© 1997 by R.C.S. Libri S.p.A., Milan
Distributed in Canada by Sterling Publishing
C/o Canadian Manda Group, One Atlantic Avenue, Suite 105
Toronto, Ontario, Canada M6K 3E7
Distributed in Great Britain and Europe by Cassell PLC
Wellington House, 125 Strand, London WC2R 0BB, England
Distributed in Australia by Capricorn Link (Australia) Pty Ltd.
P.O. Box 6651, Baulkham Hills, Business Centre, NSW 2153, Australia

Sterling ISBN 0-8069-5877-4

Paola Romanelli

COUNTRY BASKETS

Sterling Publishing Co., Inc.
New York

CONTENTS

SHAPES 69

WEAVING SUGGESTIONS 103

INTRODUCTION

When our ancestors started out to make the first baskets to hold plucked berries or to preserve seeds, they must surely have taken a close look at the patient work of birds as they built their nests, and taken a page out of their book.

The infinite variety of fibers offered by Mother Nature, and the beauty of certain knotty or colored branches provided the raw material, usually fairly easy to get, which attracted Mankind into trying his hand at weaving. It probably started off like this, as a necessity, to satisfy elementary needs, and then, with the passing of time it happened, as it does with all activities, that the techniques were improved thanks to individual powers of creativity. I think something of the kind happened to me too. As a small girl, during the long summers spent in the mountains, with nature as my real playmate, there were periods when my main activity was making containers of cyclamens. I used go into the woods looking for twigs of the same size and, having collected enough, I would get down to making a small basket.

The stubborn nature of this fiber, which often would not bend to my will, forced me to vary shapes and plans; the handle was the part least inclined to follow my desired model and my efforts achieved results not always positive. Later, when I was able to use twigs of equal size and perfect shape, weaving became a decidedly easier pleasure.

I abandoned this activity for years and took it up again when I was asked to organize a course of basket weaving.

And so it turned out that what for me had merely been a hobby became a discipline to be taught, which forced me to work out a method and operative sequences.

I need hardly say how precious this experience was when preparing this manual, which I hope will be of use for those who intend to take up this ancient " art ", which still enjoys great popularity today.

It is a good idea to use medulla at the beginning, as this is a fiber easily obtainable even in small twigs and therefore particularly pliable. For this very reason the various weaving techniques set out in this manual and the objects photographed were created with this fiber.

Paola Romanelli
paolarom@katamail.com

HISTORY OF WEAVING

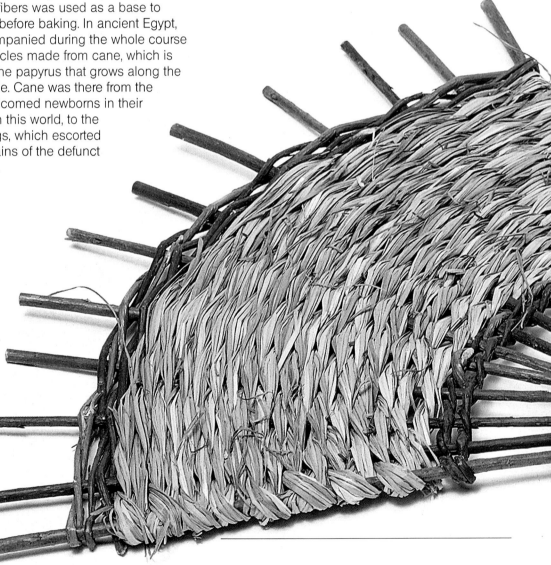

Basket weaving has prehistoric origins and existed before wool weaving and pottery-making. Thanks to the ease in obtaining the raw materials and the fact that no specific tools were required, basket weaving was practiced over a vast geographical area. Only the perishing nature of the materials used has prevented us from being able to date the origins of this craft.

The presence of basket work in ancient times is proved by findings of imprints on pottery, where the weaving of fibers was used as a base to mould the clay before baking. In ancient Egypt, man was accompanied during the whole course of his life by articles made from cane, which is obtained from the papyrus that grows along the banks of the Nile. Cane was there from the cradles that welcomed newborns in their first moments in this world, to the funeral coverings, which escorted the mortal remains of the defunct into the afterlife.

Customs and traditions connected with weaving sprang up in areas, which had a spontaneous growth of vegetation suitable for weaving. A culture within a culture occurred, a kind of patrimony of professionals who preserved and handed down know-how and tricks of the trade from generation to generation. These changed from region to region depending on the materials found there.

For example, containers produced in mountain areas were made from strong fibers such as birch, chestnut and hazel. These are fibers, which call for strong hands both in collecting and crafting them. The peasant obtained the fibers in the woods, then got them ready and wove them when he had time free from his main activities. This is all carried out with the utmost self-sufficiency and economy - he learns from the elders the various techniques down to the last secrets and then hands them down to his children in his turn. Weaving was perhaps the only form of artistic expression in the manual work of the peasants.

In other societies, such as the agro-pastoral, for example, it was the women who made the everyday household articles, often of great worth, such as cloth, weaving and embroidery. Women began as children alongside the older women, beginning from the simplest steps and going on to ever more complex techniques.

These domestic crafts were taken for granted in the past, but were considered less important than indispensable work such as carrying out the household chores and looking after the children. For this reason weaving was done during leisure hours, particularly while awaiting the men's return from the fields or from an evening out with friends. Rhythms were therefore very easy-going, it taking from a few weeks to a month to make a basket. The basket maker's work is today considered complementary because it is such a poorly paid profession. Furthermore the importation of articles from the Eastern countries, at greatly reduced cost, has lead to the progressive disappearance of this trade. Therefore, the few professionals still remaining usually just design models which are then made up in the East by a work force often consisting of mere children.

To this must be added the fact that, unlike many other crafts which have gradually been mechanized and substituted by mass production, weaving has remained exclusively manual. More sophisticated tools may be used in preparing fibers, but it is handiwork and man's sense of creativity which makes the baskets. There is a definite risk that the basket weaver's work may disappear altogether. A whole world of techniques, know-how and tricks of the trade destined to die out with the old craftsmen who now preserve them, an age-old tradition which will survive only in folk museums and in articles on "material culture".

This manual would also like to be a small contribution to preventing this ancient craft from being lost to memory.

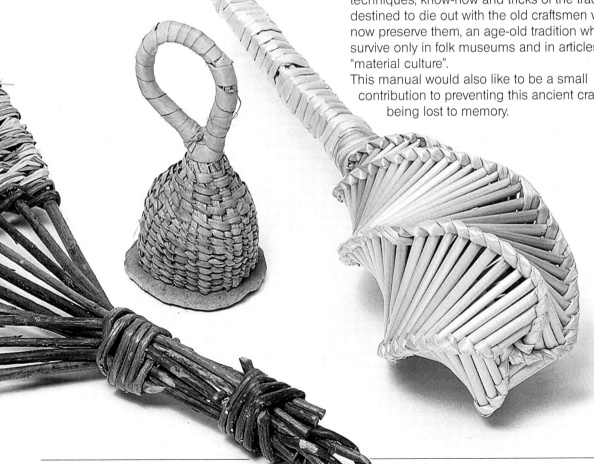

WEAVING IN THE UNITED STATES

*Caravaggio, Fruit Basket, 1599 ca., oil on canvas.
Milan, Pinacoteca Ambrosiana.*

American basket weaving has humble beginnings. It can be traced back about as for as you care to look. This is a look at the age of basketry from Native American time to modern times and how the uses have been affected by the evolution of modern tools and utensils.

Native American baskets varied from region to region, depending on the natural materials that were available in each region. The baskets that were woven served many purposes. Many were designed for gathering food and carrying personal belongings, to name a few uses. Many of the baskets, which remain today, show intricate weaving patterns and designs that amaze the most seasoned weaver today. The tedious work that went into these baskets is amazing, when one considers that they didn't have the modern equipment that we have today to prepare the materials. Some were even sealed with various natural materials to make them waterproof, so that they could be used to actually hold liquids. Some were designed to be carried on the head or fasten to the sash so the hand could be free.

The necessity and love for baskets have continued through out the ages and many of the early pioneers found baskets to be a necessity. Different styles evolved as time passed and many of those styles still exist today. Some of the different styles grew from the areas needs and can be directly associated with the regional trade. Many of the styles are still linked with their particular area today and are a part of the regional history.

Nantucket basketry is a style that had its beginnings on the Island of Nantucket and remains a rich part of the history there. This type of basket is woven over a wooden mold and uses a slotted base, which could have been made of various woods. Some intricate ones have scrimshaw work adorning them as well as some of the antique ones containing ivory pieces as well. This comes from the fact that Nantucket was once, almost exclusively, a whaling community.

Shaker basketry came from the Shakers who came to the U.S. from England in the late 1770's. Their contributions to history include their basket style and furniture.

Rib basketry styles are a very old type, which can be dated back to at least the days of the pioneers. These were used mainly for the collection of eggs. The style allowed the basket to carry many eggs without the risk of breakage. The rib construction made a strong basket with the weight distribution, as such; it protected the eggs from cracking under the weight.

As time passed and we developed more modern materials, such as plastics and variations of all kinds of metal types, which already existed, basketry as a necessity did continue until the new materials became more commonplace and financially feasible. Out of convenience, we turned to the newer alternatives. Plastics are more durable, and were looked upon as the wave of the future as a modern alternative. Baskets became more of an

ornamental item used for decoration. They were no longer a necessity.

Many of the antique baskets are quite expensive in many parts of the US. They seem to be a favored item of many antique collectors these days.

Basketry is one of the few art forms that have not been completely taken over by the machine industry. There is still no machine that can do the actual process of weaving. This remains a process, which must be done by hand.

The history of basketry has evolved into what we have today. Many of us now look upon basketry as an art form from a past era and we marvel at its history. If you look around at the items we use in everyday life, you will be surprised at how many of

us use baskets. The next time you are in a restaurant, take notice of what the bread or crackers are served in. Stores use them for display purposes, and sometimes as shopping baskets. Young girls use them to hold hair clips and cosmetics.

Industry has answered the large need for weaving materials, with importers bringing in mass amounts of rattan from several countries abroad to fill the needs of the weavers in this country as well as many other countries. The rattan is processed in other countries and brought here for resale and basketry has not only remained alive, but has grown into a large' community', so to speak.

Many weavers still find the time to choose their

own hard woods and process their materials by hand themselves, by pounding trees to separate the growth rings and using drawl blades to make the weaving splints. Although the process from start to finish is much longer, the rewards upon completion are tremendous. There are several communities that have a base of basketry. Dresden, Ohio is a prime example. It is a basketry-based community. The tourism that is created by the

Longerberger factory is unbelievable.

Basketry has grown over the past years and has become huge, for lack of a better word. Basketry is being taught in formal classroom settings in some of the technical schools and independent instructors offer classes across the country. This has lead to the formation of basketry guilds, which have annual conventions, seminars, and weave-ins. They do

their best to keep everyone interested up to date with the latest information on tools, materials, patterns and all other information that might relate. Some of the collectors have hundreds of baskets in their collections. Some prefer antique ones and some don't care, they label themselves 'basket cases' and collect and all they can get.

There seem to be trendy swings in basketry, as there are in most everything from fashion to cars, and the trend as we prepare to enter the new millennium is the return to natural fibers. That is basically gathering any weavable fiber, which grows naturally, and using them to weave. Some people even raise specific plants to use in their weavings. Grapevine, willow and most any other vine plant can be used.

With the development of the Internet, the lines of communication have opened even more. Weaving networks have opened up there as well. There are many great resources available. Some have forums so you can trade valuable information with other weavers. With technology growing as it is, if you are interested in basketry, the resources are available.

WEAVING THROUGHOUT THE WORLD

Weaving techniques are in use all over the world. Millions of people who live in societies where mass production is not yet widespread make daily us of objects created by weaving fibers together. These range from houses to children's playthings, from furnishings to clothing, from games to hundreds of containers for carrying the most diverse products.

In the Far East, more than anywhere else in the world, woven goods are produced, thanks to the presence there of numerous vegetable species. China, in particular, is characterized by an enormous production both for local use and, over the last few decades, for the Western market. Today, in fact, the greater part of woven goods sold in Italy, for example, is "Made in China". The skill and versatility of Chinese craftsmen allows them to produce not only traditional articles but also products to order for the West, at very competitive costs but at a high quality level.

In other parts of Asia, Africa or America, the craft of weaving, though widespread at local level, is of no importance for exports and is limited to internal trade, when not just actually a non-commercial family business.

Let's have a detailed look at how basket weaving is characterized in the various geographic areas. From the Amazon to the Far East, the use of panels made from reeds or other fibers woven or

fixed to a frame is widespread. These are employed as walls for cabins which, assembled together, take on different characteristics according to the place. In Mali, for example, a panel of woven fibers constitutes a rough cabin in itself. Inclined and held up by one sole stick, it is generally used as a protection from the sun. Mats of varying size can be found covering the floors of Chinese houses or Mosques in Tunisia. Change scenario, and the mats are now the pallets in Peruvian cabins or are used for sitting on or displaying goods by tradesmen in Senegal. Along tropical rivers they are placed as canopies or roofing on boats to protect passengers from the sun and rain. In some countries, matting substitutes for fabric or carton for wrapping various goods. Shoulder panniers can be found practically everywhere. The shape, more or less conical, and the type of fiber may vary. For populations who have no beasts of burden available and are not motorized they still

constitute the most used containers for carrying large and cumbersome burdens.

What differs from continent to continent is the manner in which these panniers are held. In the East, they are held by a strip of fabric encircling the head. In America, small-sized baskets are wrapped in a piece of cloth (manta) and carried on the chest. In Africa, where it is not the custom to carry burdens on one's shoulders, baskets are carried directly on the head, if necessary fitting a rolled up sheet beneath the basket to get a better balance. In Europe, panniers with two shoulder straps throw all the weight onto the shoulders. In this way people manage to carry earth products, stones, coal, wood and a host of other goods for miles. In Nepal, where they lack roads, carriers transport the sick on a kind of sedan chair placed on the shoulders and supported, as is the custom, by a band around the head. In the East, it is very common to see pairs of baskets tied at the extremities of a balancing pole poised on one or both shoulders. These contain all sorts of things, including animals and babies. Weaving is also very much used to make pack-saddles for donkeys and dromedaries. In Peru, in the Persian Gulf, and in the marshes of Italy, boats were built with strips of woven vegetables. The essence used naturally varied, but the shape and length of the boats, between ten to fourteen feet long, were very similar. In Mexico, Egypt and Indonesia, wide-meshed baskets are used for carrying chicken, geese, and fighting cocks. These types of weaving are sometimes

not quite baskets, but rather a sort of cage that can be raised when necessary.

Naturally, smaller-sized baskets are used practically all over the world for picking or displaying local products. Circular-shaped baskets are definitely the most popular ones, but the materials and techniques used to make them vary considerably from country to country. In the Far East, a wide array of household objects in wickerwork, such as beds, armchairs, cradles, shelves, lampshades, trunks, etc, can be found in most homes. Other objects, which are simpler to make, such as trays, baskets for storing vegetables, sieves, and colanders, are used in places where food is stored and prepared. In Morocco it is the custom to store bread in baskets with conical lids. In the Sahel Zone, baskets are often replaced by large containers made of emptied pumpkins and covered with lids made of simple, flat-shaped spiral wickerwork. This is not to mention the variety of boxes and caskets available, from the simpler parallelepiped-shaped ones with reeds to the more elaborate ones, painted and decorated with the varnishes typical of some regions in India. In the Sahel, boxes are made with a mixed technique, i.e. with emptied pumpkins, vegetable fibers and strips of leather. In Birmania and Thailand, cylindrical or round containers are made by weaving horsehair, subsequently lacquered and decorated with natural colors in the tones of orange and green. In Mexico, it is possible to find net-woven bags of rope or with rigid sisal fibers sometimes decorated with strong hues. China produces suitcases and rigid bags made in wicker or with reeds, while Indonesia makes refined cylindrical backpacks so woven with different-colored fibers as to highlight their geometrical and decorative shapes. Though less common, there is also an array of clothing accessories in wickerwork. They range from the traditional Latin American broad-rimmed hats, to the conic or bell-shaped ones made with reeds and used by peasants in the Far East, to the headgear peculiar to the people of Sahel: circular, broad-rimmed hats made with rough fibers and leather decorations. Sandals, belts, decorative harnesses, fans and purses complete the range of products, which are woven and worn in some countries. And then there are the toys, such as the dolls and puppets made in Sri Lanka, the shapes of animals woven with palm leaves by Moroccan children, and the Peruvian boats made with totora fibers.

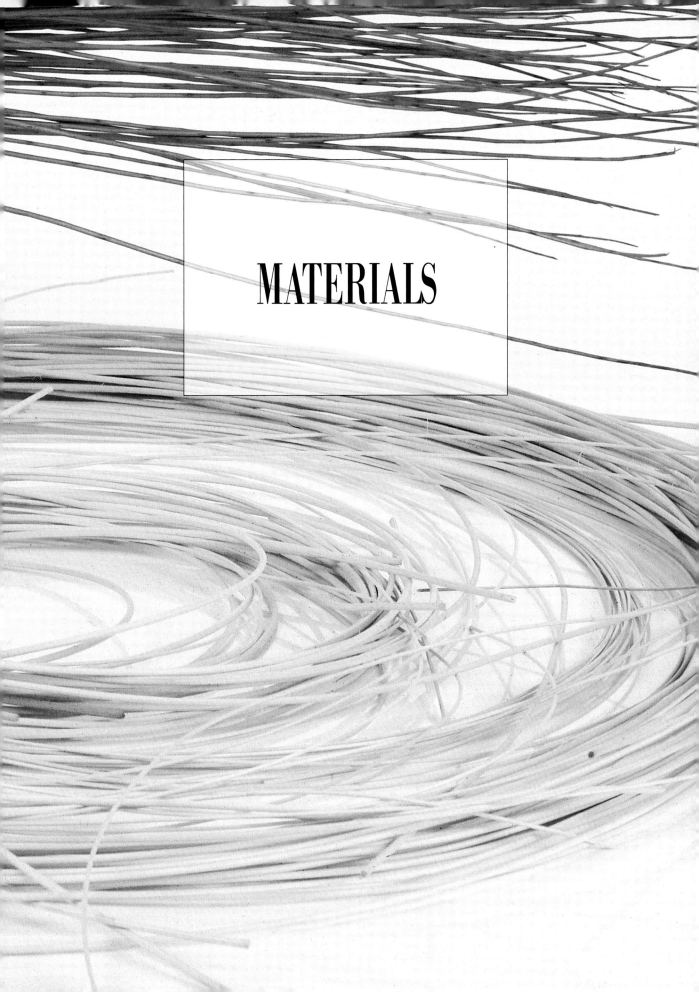

MATERIALS

THE FIBERS

Some common fibers, such as wicker and medulla are available on the market. However, if you penetrate into a wood, walk along the banks of a waterway or follow a path in the countryside, you can find a wide range of arboreous species, many of which offer fibers, which lend themselves well to wickerwork. Learning to recognize these fibers will come in useful for those of you who wish to procure the material yourselves, it will help you choose the more appropriate texture and color, and will naturally save you money. Outlined below is an in-depth account of the fibers that lend themselves best to wickerwork.

REEDS

The reed is a herbaceous plant pertaining to the Giungacee family, which comprises several hundred species. It is very common in marshlands, along the riverbanks and lakesides, as well as along the seacoasts because it tolerates a high concentration of salt. It grows in all the humid areas in Europe. Its cylindrical leaves, which can be several meters long, are excellent material for weaving work (*Juncus*, from the Latin *iungere*, i.e. to tie).
The best period to pick this plant is during the summer months when it is in its full vegetative cycle, just when inflorescence begins to dry. It is important that the season be hot so that the culms, monocotyledonous stems (as of a grass or sedge), have time to desiccate in the sun. There are three important operations to follow when picking this plant. First, the culms must be picked one at a time from within the bush. Secondly, the culms must be chosen according to their different lengths, dividing them into two groups, the long and the short ones (the latter are the best and are used for more refined work); Finally, defibration must be made by way of torsion. The last phase consists in drying and preserving the faggots. Reeds must be spread out in wide, sunny areas (roofs and terraces) and the minute they start to yellow, must be tied into faggots and stored in dry places such as lofts, haylofts or barns. While they are being worked, reed must be rehydrated and this is why we recommend you sprinkle water over them with a watering can. Once this operation has been carried out, cover the reeds in a damp cloth for a couple of hours, after which you can start weaving it.

CANE

The word "cane" indicates the stems of some species of creeping herbaceous plants such as *Calamus* which grow in a vast area of the African, Indian, Malaysian and Chinese tropical belt. The picking and preparation of cane is carried out by hand by numerous people. It is cut and deprived of its external, hairier layer. The stem, which is thin and flexible, is reduced to strips and used to seat chairs, for example. The central part, treated industrially, is reduced to different-sized branches and can be found at wholesalers in faggots of different width commonly known as medulla and rattan. Cane is easy to work with in that it lends itself very well to weaving. It is either hay color or whitish.
Cane must be rehydrated, therefore immerse it in water for ten minutes or so. In this way the fiber will regain its elasticity and become more moldable. Make sure, however, not to leave it in water for too long. Water will ruin the fiber by exfoliating and darkening it.

WICKER

This name come from the Latin *Vimen* which means to weave.
By wicker, it is meant the young and flexible branches pertaining to some species of willow trees (*Salix Viminalis*, *Salix purpurea*, *Salix trianda*),

Faggot of natural wicker

Skein of medulla

with gray and cracked bark, which grow along the waterways. They are often cultivated in vineyards by peasants who use the more slender branches for tying vine shoots together.

In winter, when the plant's vegetative cycle is over, the younger branches of the year underway are uprooted. They are then prepared in different manners. One way consists in keeping the bark and desiccating the fiber until it turns from green to brown. Its look is rather rustic and it is generally used to make untreated baskets. Another way consists in boiling the branches instead so that the tannin is contained in the bark dyes the wood below, the bark is then stripped. The fiber is therefore darker, but more uniform and can be used to make refined objects. A third way consists in leaving the branches in water the whole winter and stripping the bark in spring, when the fibers have turned a paler color.

Fibers gathered in faggots vary in length from 40" to 82" (1 to 2.5 meters) and often vary in width (the fiber presents a part of greater width, which decreases towards the summit). In order to work the fibers, they must be rehydrated, in other words they must be left in water for 1 to 3-4 hours according to their length. After which they must be kept damp, wrapped in a wet cloth until weaving actually commences. To prevent the wicker from becoming slimy, do not keep it wrapped in the wet cloth for too long.

ASPHODEL

Asphodel is a herbaceous plant pertaining to the Liliaceous family (*Asphodelus ramosus*). Its stem (scape) is a little over three feet high and supports a white or yellow inflorescence in clusters, with long leaves. In Ancient Greece and Rome, this plant was sacred to the dead.

It dries in the summer and blooms in the autumn, and this determines the picking period. The scape, the part used for weaving, is considered ripe when it supports flowers which are still in the bud, just before they blossom.

PALMETTO

The Palmetto (*Chamaerops humilis*) is typical of hot countries and is widespread along the whole Mediterranean coast. Its cylindrical stem is very short and woody, and is surmounted by a tuft of big, flexible pinnate or rayed leaves. The fibers of this kind of palm are used for horsehair and brushes, and in particular ropes used both in agriculture and in the Navy. Palmetto is picked in summer, generally during the hottest hours when the fibers offer less resistance to being cut.

RAFFIA

Raffia (*Raphia ruffia*) is a type of palm typical of the tropical regions. It has a short trunk and long, pinnate leaves. Soft, robust fibers are obtained from the median ribs if these leaves.

BEFORE BEGINNING

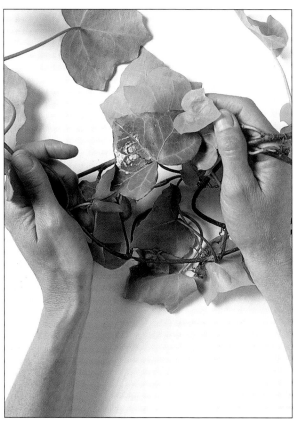

If you are thinking of procuring the fibers yourselves, remember that branches must be picked between October and March, when the vegetative cycle of the plant is over and lymphs are no longer present in the veins. Choose branches from the current year. Choose branches which are neither too rigid nor too woody, but if possible straight and slender. Procure some branches with pinecones, berries, or buds, and others with characteristic barks and small lichens. Then try to bend a branch around your fist: if it does not break, it is perfect for your wickerwork. Now cut the branches with a pair of sharp shears, making sure you leave some leaf-buds on the plant for the following year.

If you prefer vivid colors, wait until the January frosts are over to pick the branches: in this period, your wishes will be fulfilled. Most of the species require a two or three-week seasoning before they can be used. Therefore purchase a pair of leather gardening gloves and prepare the branches one by one before tying them in bunches. It is always necessary to remove the leaves from evergreen and holly plants and to do this easily, simply rub your gloved hand down the stem.

Some species, such as dog roses, are covered in thorns. To remove them, again rub your gloved hand up and down the stem. The small leaves of creeping plants such as ivy can be preserved, in other words prevented from drying, by immersing them in glycerin and water for 4 or 5 days. Other creeping plants, such as honeysuckle and clematis, can easily be deprived of their herbaceous barks by arranging them in a wreath and boiling them a little in an old pot. While picking the fibers, try and think of how to make the handles: hazel and chestnut branches the size of a finger will do fine. Bend them delicately in the form of an arch and, tie their ends and leave them to dry for some weeks, even without their bark. Bunch the newly picked fibers together, divided per species, and leave them to season for two or three weeks (it is up to you to understand when they are sufficiently elastic to be treated).

If too much time passes from when the fibers were first picked, they will need to be rehydrated for a couple of hours and must be kept wrapped in a wet cloth the whole night long. If instead you think that some newly picked fibers are suitable for immediate wickerwork, then give them a try.

Below is a list of the most common trees suitable for basket weaving found in temperate climates:

Maple, Holly, Birch, Honeysuckle, Cherry-tree, Clematis, Cotton, Cornel-tree, Ivy, Eucalyptus, Forsythia, Ash, Jasmine, Broom, Wisteria, Larch, Bay, Privet, Magnolia, Hazel, Elm, Alder, Passionflower, Periwinkle, Thorn Bush, Oak, Dog Rose, Weeping Willow, Yew, Lime, Vine.

DYEING

breaking while weaving, but must be immersed several times in the dye until it assumes the color desired. The colors obtained from these materials are soft, very delicate ones. This will give your basket an "old style" look. With this same technique its is possible to use a dye made from tea, saffron or turmeric. If you decide to use these materials, first melt the powders in hot water. When the water has reached the color desired, dip in the fibers. Afterwards, rinse them in cold water.

If you feel like working with colored fibers, then it is interesting to know that both cane and wicker lend themselves very well to dyeing. It is possible to dye individual fibers or the whole basket, but the latter is quite risky because during the boiling phase the basket frame may come undone and some fastenings be loosened.

Given that baskets are often used as food containers, remember to employ non-toxic products. It is possible to create dyes with natural products such as berries, nuts, acorns, barks, etc. If these products are employed, then the fiber must be rolled up well and immersed for short intervals in a pan of boiling water. It is advisable to use rainwater in which, closed in a cloth bag or an old sock, you have put some nuts, berries or bark to boil. The fiber itself must not be boiled in order to prevent it from becoming fragile and

instead, it is possible to purchase the powders used for dying fabric directly from paint shops. These dyes usually come in small sachets and in an extremely wide array of colors. If you have trouble in dipping wicker in these dyes, given that it is impossible to roll into skeins, you can always use the plastic tubes used in the building trade. Stoppered by corks generally used for demijohns, these tubes can hold the dyes and fibers in all their length. Remember to shake the tube constantly so that the color is uniform.

Another way of obtaining soft colors is by using food colorings, i.e. natural, edible compounds, which are available in drugstores. These food colorings must be diluted in water and boiled. Fibers are always dyed by way of immersion. If you wish to obtain strong, contrasting colors

TOOLS

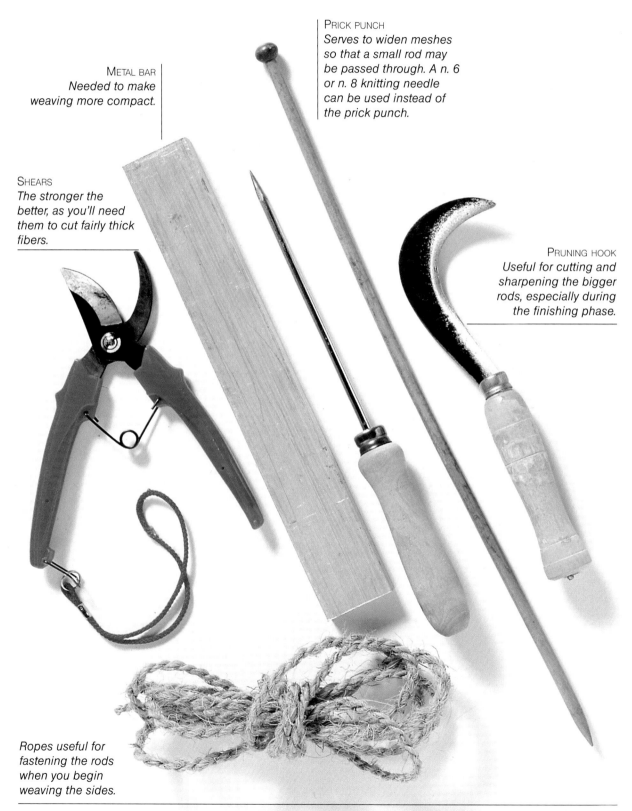

PRICK PUNCH
Serves to widen meshes so that a small rod may be passed through. A n. 6 or n. 8 knitting needle can be used instead of the prick punch.

METAL BAR
Needed to make weaving more compact.

SHEARS
The stronger the better, as you'll need them to cut fairly thick fibers.

PRUNING HOOK
Useful for cutting and sharpening the bigger rods, especially during the finishing phase.

Ropes useful for fastening the rods when you begin weaving the sides.

GREASE
Grease, which can be replaced by soap, is used to facilitate working with the prick punch. It is generally found in the cavity of a bone.

MEASURING TAPE
Necessary for measuring the length of the rods.

PEGS
May come in handy for blocking some weaving rods during work.

VAPORIZER
Useful for dampening the fibers.

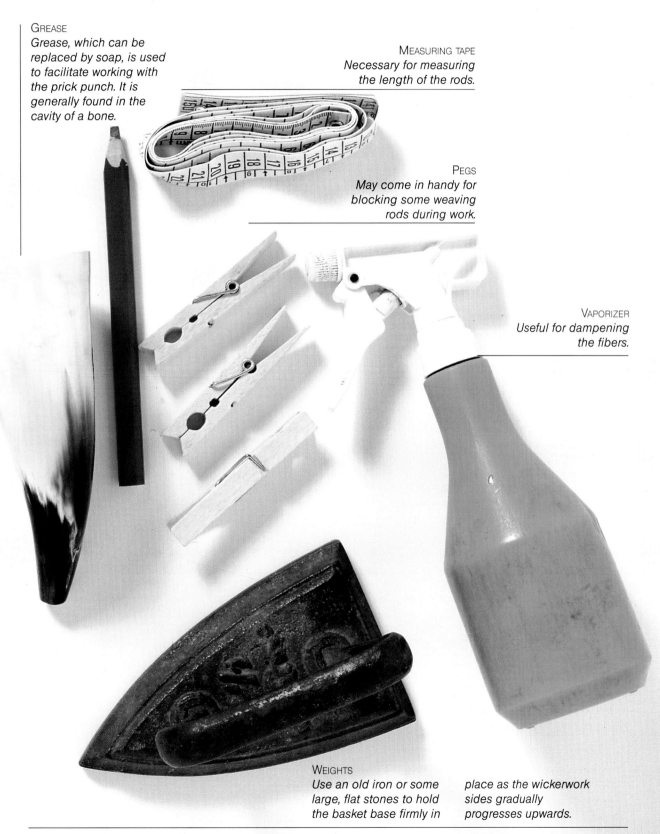

WEIGHTS
Use an old iron or some large, flat stones to hold the basket base firmly in place as the wickerwork sides gradually progresses upwards.

TECHNIQUE

DESIGNING A BASKET

The most important thing is to decide what kind of basket one wants to design. I always find that it is a good idea to sketch the chosen model on a sheet of paper and to roughly decide its dimensions because the length of the rods is determined by the size of the basket being made. The size of the rods needed to make a basket is arrived at by the sum of the length (or diameter) of the base plus the double of the length of the sides

plus 12" (6" per side). As regards the fiber width, the rods are usually bigger than the weaving rod, although this is at you discretion because it depends on what you intend the basket for. There is no correct weaving position: some use a table as their work space, others prefer to hold the basket on their lap, still others prefer to sit on a low stool and keep the basket on the floor.

To maintain the fibers damp during work place them in plastic bags.

Remember, however, to wet the fibers and to keep them damp while working. In fact, if you notice that your basket is becoming dry, then immerse it completely in water so that it regains the necessary elasticity. It is advisable to keep a garden vaporizer handy at all times.

MAKING A BASKET

To make these projects medulla fiber was used as it is the easiest to weave. For this first, simple basket, the fiber width, both for the rod and the weaving rod measures 1/8" (3 mm). The base is circular and has an 8" (20 cm) wide diameter, while the sides are 4" (10 cm) high. The length of the rods measure 28" (70 cm). The length of the weaving rods is always that of the faggot from which they have been taken.

ROUND BASES

Cut eight rods 28" (70 cm) long and mark them half way with a pencil.

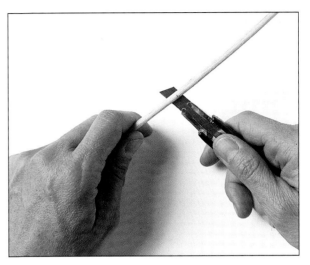

With the help of a very sharp cutting knife make a cut in the center of the fiber lengthwise about 1" (3 cm) long, exactly over the half-way mark.
Repeat this operation on four rods.

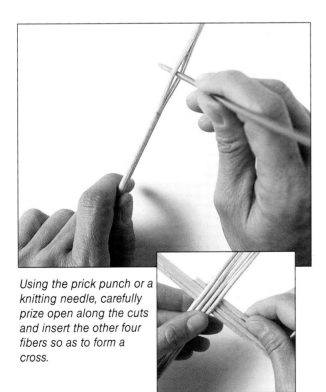

Using the prick punch or a knitting needle, carefully prize open along the cuts and insert the other four fibers so as to form a cross.

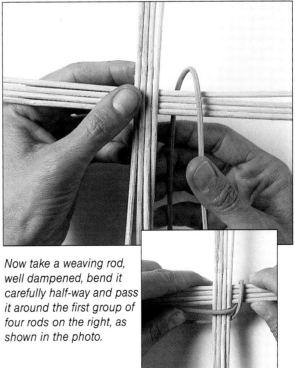

Now take a weaving rod, well dampened, bend it carefully half-way and pass it around the first group of four rods on the right, as shown in the photo.

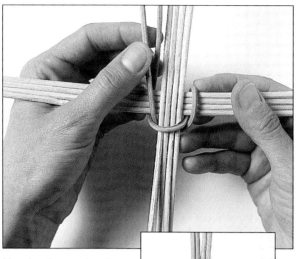

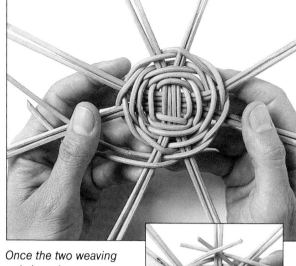

Now begin weaving the two-element plait. Cross the two ends of the weaving rod passing one over and the other under the second group of four rods (weave clockwise). Continue for three complete rounds. Separate the groups of four rods into groups of two and carry on weaving.

Once the two weaving rods have been completed, substitute them with another two at the same time. Hold the end of one of the weaving rods towards the top part of the base and place the new one alongside it. Try to secure it by weaving the end part of the second weaving rod.

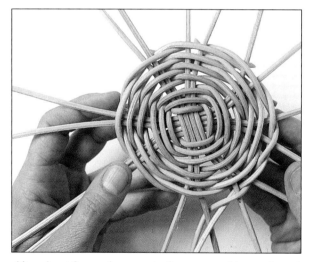

After about 3 rounds separate the groups of two rods and continue with the over-under technique. Check that the rods are well arranged in rays, with equal distance between them.

Be sure the spiral proceeds regularly until the desired size of the base has been reached.
While working, be sure that the weaving rods do not slacken by putting a certain pressure on them, so that the weaving turns out compact and no gaps remain between one fiber and another.

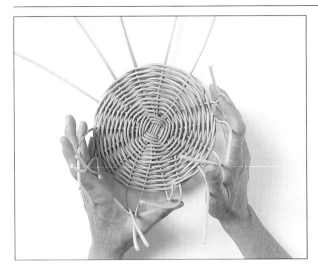

Secure the ends of the weaving rods by inserting them in the weaving of the previous round, alongside a rod.

The base may now be turned right side up. Dampen the rods well and bend them upwards, tying them with a string. Place some weights on the base of the basket in order to keep it steady.

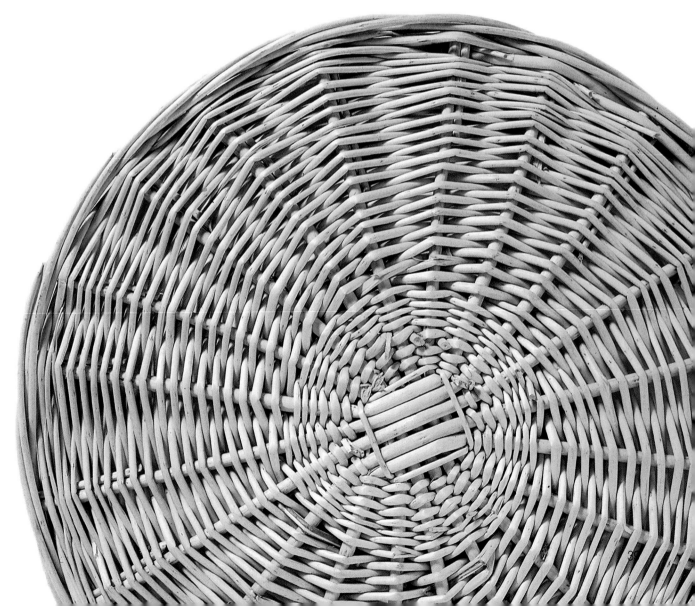

THE SIDES

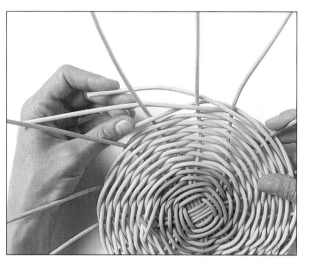

You may now proceed to weaving with three weaving rods to make the sides. Work is carried out inside the basket, from left to right.

Take three weaving rods and insert their end inside the next three rods. Each weaving rod passes from left to right over two rods and under one. Repeat these steps for about 4" (10 cm).

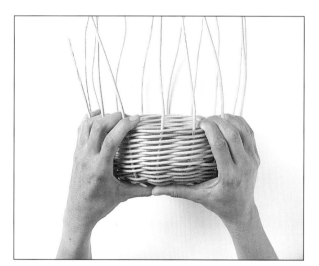

Check the shape of the basket continually and, where necessary, press the rods and keep the weaving taut so that the basket will have the desired shape

A metal bar could also be used to give the weaving rods light blows from top to bottom between one rod and another, so as to make the weaving more compact. When the three weaving rods are finished secure them inside the basket, behind each rod, in the weaving of the previous round. If the work has been carried out with precision, a spiral form can be noticed inside the basket.

THE BORDER

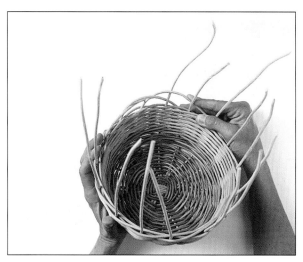

The border is made by bending each rod towards the right inside the following one and leaving its end towards the outside of the basket.

Each rod then returns to the inside of the basket, passing through the eyelet, which has formed in the fold of the neighboring rod.

It then returns outside, passing inside the next rod. Continue for the entire length of the rods. At the end, the last one is woven under the others. The rods must finish inside the basket.

When the basket weaving has been finished, the next step is the clipping. With sharp shears cut the ends of the weaving rods diagonally.

OVAL BASE

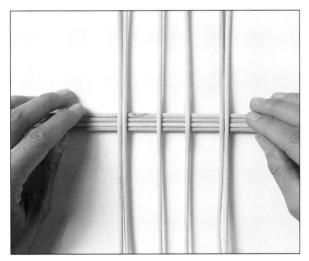

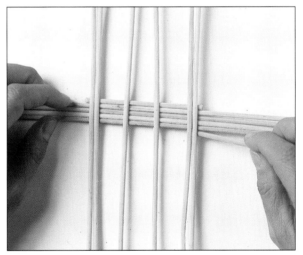

Cut 10 or more rods of a certain length to create this basket of the size desired. Mark 6 of them halfway with a pencil, then with the cutter make a cut big enough to insert the other 4 rods.
Put the cut rods 1 1/4" (3 cm) apart, pairing the first two and the last two.

Now cut two rods 3" (9 cm) long (or as long as the distance between the first and the last) and insert them at the two sides of the previous four rods so as to prevent the base from twisting.

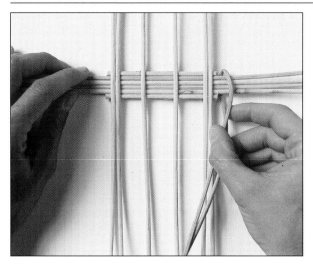

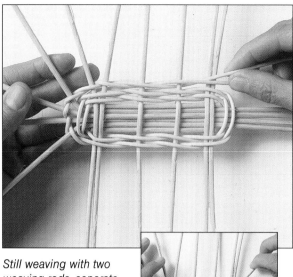

Take a weaving rod, which should be smaller than the rods (1/16" – 2 mm), damp it and bend it in half. Pass it around the four side rods on the right and weave their two ends, passing one over and the other under the rods clockwise. Make two more complete rounds.

Still weaving with two weaving rods, separate the rods at the sides, placing them in rays. Now insert another rod from one side, half as long as the previous ones, in order to obtain an uneven number.

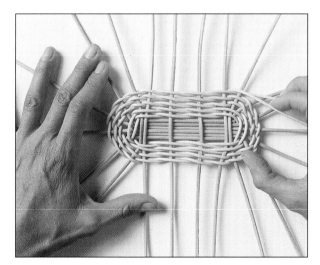

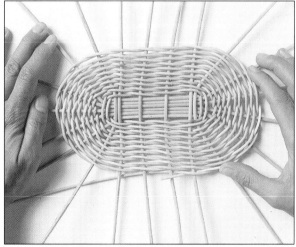

Weaving the curves presents the greatest difficulty, as the fibers tend to separate. Continue weaving, after having changed the weaving rod for a bigger one [3/32" (3 mm) or 2/16" (4 mm)], until the desired size has been reached.

The bigger the base, the easier it will loose its shape, therefore dampen it well when finished and dry it under a weight of a few kilos. When the rods have been bent upwards 90° you can begin work on the sides.

SQUARE BASE

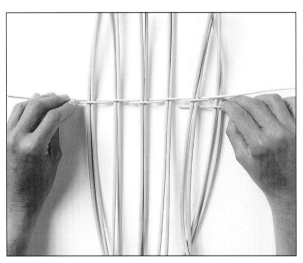

Cut 12 or more rods of the desired length. Place them on a flat surface in twos, at about 1" from each other. Take a weaving rod smaller than the rods and of the desired length and, beginning from the left, pass it under and over each pair of rods.

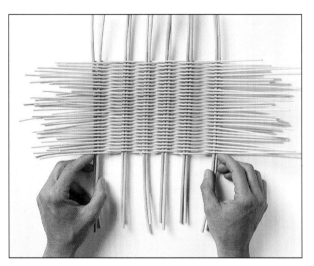

Take another weaving rod, the same as the previous one, and weave under-over in the opposite direction to the previous round.
Continue until the required size has been reached.

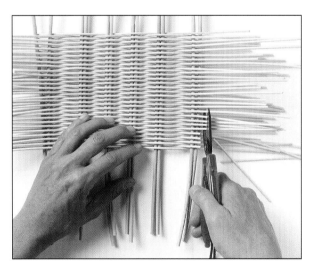

With the shears now cut all the ends of the weaving rods that face upwards both on the right and on the left.

Dampen the work and bend upwards in a right angle the ends both of the weaving rods and of the rods.
You are now ready to weave the sides.

The main characteristic of this large, roll-holding basket is the dividing panel, fastened at the same point as the handle.

WEAVING THE SIDES

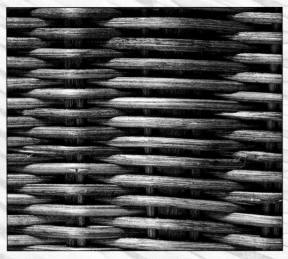

This is an example of simple weaving carried out with one sole weaving rod. The fiber used is medulla, dyed with fabric colors.

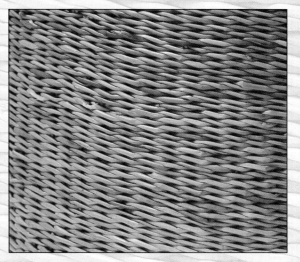

Diagonal weaving with the number of weaving rods equaling that of the rods, and carried out in a natural colored, very thin fiber.

The bunches of weaving rods are united here by rods which bind them with a diagonal motif. The result is a very strong basket.

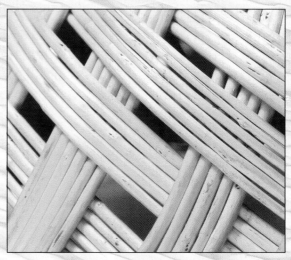

The weaving rods and the rods, both in medulla of the same size are woven diagonally, passing over two groups of fiber and under one.

Strips of cane are woven diagonally, leaving the mesh quite large, which gives the work a light touch.

Both the weaving rods and the rods are here made up of wide strips of chestnut wood, woven at right angles. This makes an ideal rustic basket.

Here the weaving rods are woven diagonally. Among the wide corn stalk fibers one can see the rods made from robust hazel branches.

This is a simple, regular type of weaving from medulla. Each rod is made from a pair of medulla fibers.
A coat of linseed oil, passed over the basket surface, brightens the color somewhat and prevents it from being damaged with use.

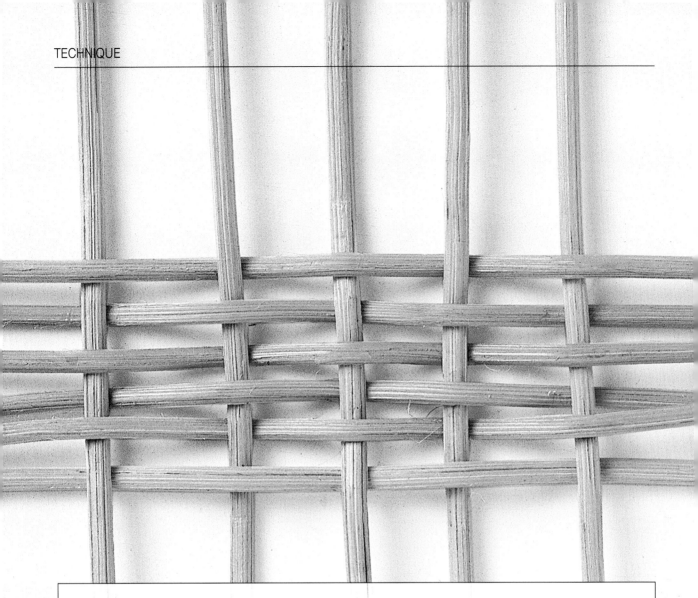

SIMPLE WEAVING

This is worked by passing a weaving rod first inside and then outside the rods forming the basket's side frame.
This is continued until the whole fiber has been used up, and another is added beginning from the rod where the first one finished. The rods must be uneven in number.

DOUBLE WEAVING

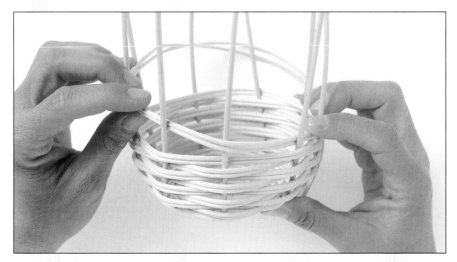

Pass a pair of weaving rods inside and outside the rods, which form the basket frame. Here too the rods must be uneven in number.

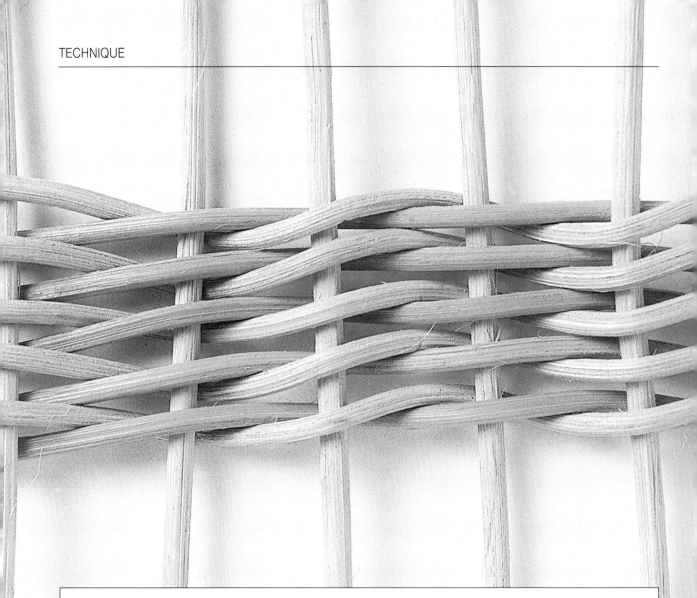

WEAVING WITH TWO PLAITED WEAVING RODS

The two ends of the weaving rods are crossed, with one passing inside and the other outside the rods forming the basket's side frame.

WEAVING WITH THREE PLAITED WEAVING RODS

This consists in weaving three weaving rods. Each of these passes inside for two consecutive rods and outside for one. If the number of rods is even, a spiral will be formed inside the basket. If uneven, the spiral will be outside.

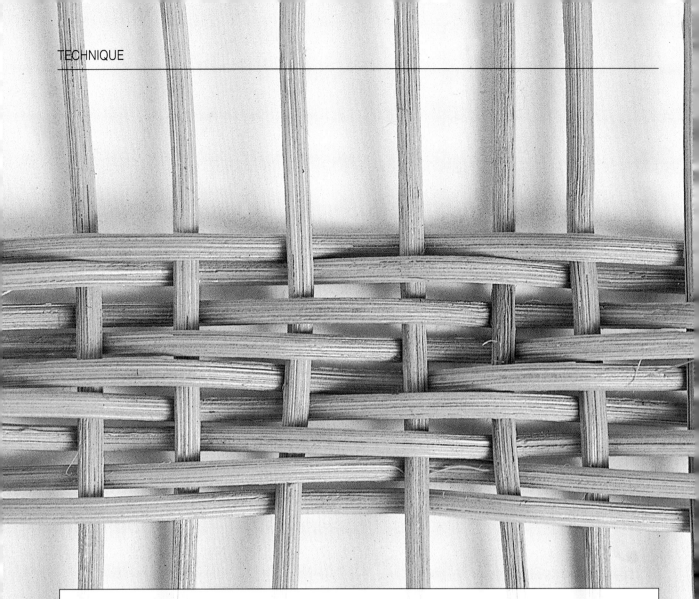

DIAGONAL WEAVING WITH TWO WEAVING RODS

Just one weaving rod is woven at a time, with an even number of rods. The weaving rod passes inside for one rod and outside for two.

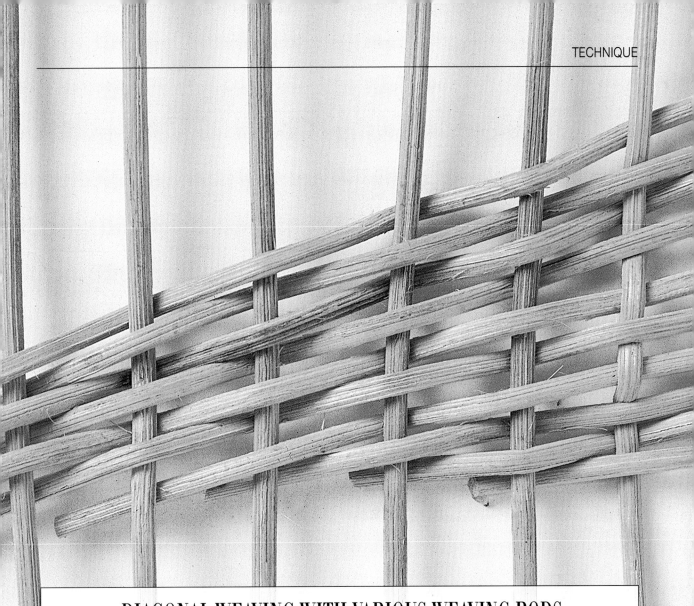

DIAGONAL WEAVING WITH VARIOUS WEAVING RODS

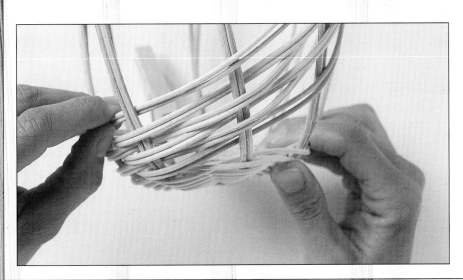

Each begins at the base of the basket and is fastened inside at a point corresponding with a rod and passed inside and outside with a diagonal trend which begins at the base and proceeds to the top border. The second weaving rod, starting from the next rod, follows the first and so on.

WEAVING THE BORDER

A plait is the best type of border for finishing off a basket, but because it is rather hard to do, we advise trying it after having practiced simpler models.

The border fibers are woven in a twist and secured at the last round by the sides through tying one of the weaving rod used for the border.

The weaving rods are woven in a twist around the basket. In this example, the fibers used are the same used in weaving the sides.

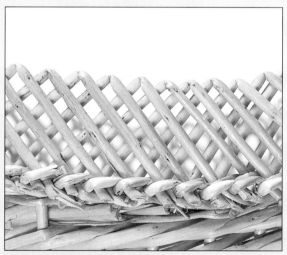

The weaving rods of this particular border are raised by about 2" (5 cm). Over the last round of the sides, and then folded at 90 degrees towards the bottom until they connect with the basket fibers.

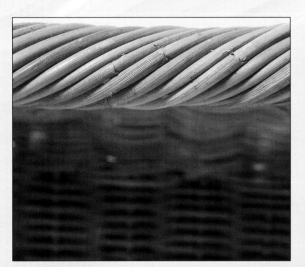

The big fibers of this basket are woven together in a twist using the last two rounds of the sides as a base. The difficulty of the border lies in avoiding leaving empty spaces between one fiber and another.

In this example, the weaving rods have been woven together so as to form a small, simple plait. Then, instead of finishing the work inside the basket, the fibers are left on the outside and all cut to the same length.

This simple border is decorated by weaving a fine, flexible branch of larch with some pinecones. Care must be taken when working not to damage them.

This small basket too is decorated in the last round of weaving the side with a branch of alder tree gathered during the budding period.

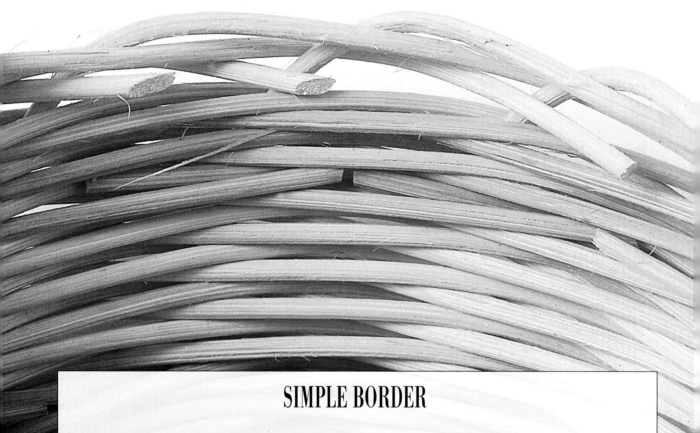

SIMPLE BORDER

Damper the rods well. Sharpen the ends and fold each rod in an arch.

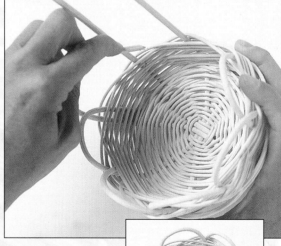

Insert the ends as far as the base beside the next rod, using a punch if necessary. Repeat these steps, crossing each rod with the following one. Though simple to make, it is not easy to manage arches of the same size.

STRONG BORDER

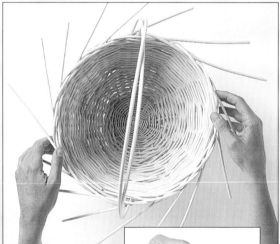

In this type of border, each rod, well dampened, is folded at right angles and is woven by passing inside and outside the successive rods, which make up the sides. You will find some difficulty with the last three rods, which are hard to weave with the first three. The weaving will have to be a little slack at the beginning to make space for the last rods.

When the work is finished, you can make the weaving more taut and thread the protruding ends to the inside of the basket in oblique fashion.

PLAITING

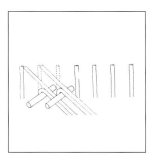

1. Procure 3 rods (S1, S2, S3) the same size as those of the basket, and two short sticks (B1, B2), to mark the start of the work. Bend the first and second rod at right angles. Place two rods (S1 and S2) alongside and pass them over and under the sticks (B1, B2).

2. Delicately bend the first pair of rods over the second and in front of the third rod, entering the basket behind the fourth.

3. Bend the third rod at right angles with S3 alongside, and pass the pair over the first pair. You will now have two pairs outside and one inside the basket.

4. Delicately bend the second pair of rods over the third, in front of the fourth, and enter the basket behind the fifth. You will now have one pair outside and one inside the basket.

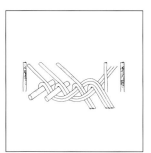

5. Bend the fourth rod at right angles together with the first pair, which will return outside the basket. You will now have three rods together. In the next step leave aside the first additional rod (S1), which must be cut at the end.

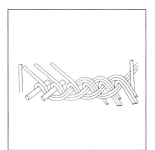

6. Continue to work round in circles until you find yourselves back at the starting point, as indicated in step n. 5.

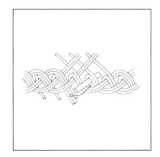

7. Now remove the two short sticks used at the beginning (B1 and B2) and weave the two previous pairs, which will enter the basket through the eyelet.

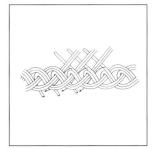

8. Secure the three rods added at the beginning of the work (S1, S2, S3), bending them to the left and inserting them in the split under the border, on the front of the basket.

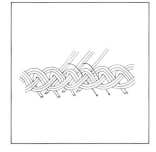

9. Let the entire plait slide through your fingers to make the your work uniform. Make sure there are no crossed or knotted fibers. Lastly, bend the three remaining rods at 90° towards the inside, and weave them through the slits towards the outside. Now cut the ends so that they are hidden under the border of the plait.

HANDLE-MAKING

The weaving rods which form this handle are secured to the top border of the basket with a taut, ring-shaped fastening of the same fiber used for both the handle and the border.

This small handle is a robust one. It is made with a considerable number of weaving rods that are the same width as the side frame. It helps when carrying a large basket.

A curved strip of wood a few inches thick was used to finish off this basket with a rustic handle. The latter was secured outside the side frames with two fastenings per side.

The branch of a hazel tree, devoid of its bark, was bent to a 'U' shape, left to dry for several weeks and fastened in the side frames through its tips purposely sharpened.

ROBUST HANDLE

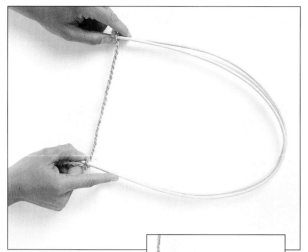

Procure two of the biggest rods you have, moisten them and give them a "U" shape. Tie their ends with a piece of string and leave to dry for a couple of days. Sharpen the ends of the rods with a pruning hook.

Insert the ends of the handle in the sides of the basket, next to the diametrically opposed side rods, if necessary using a knitting needle. The radius of the arch formed by the handle must measure about 8" (20 cm).

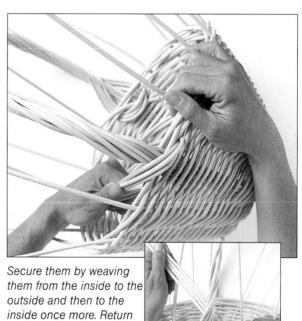

Take four weaving rods, sharpen their extremities the way you have just done for the other rods and insert then in the sides next to the two previous rods. Wet the weaving rods and twist them around the two rods clockwise. Make sure that they are side by side and do not overlap one another. You must reach the opposite side of the handle.

Secure them by weaving them from the inside to the outside and then to the inside once more. Return to the starting point, interlacing in the empty spaces. If you don't cover all the empty spaces you can add another weaving rod. Secure the work by passing the four weaving rods around the handle and threading them in the sides.

SMALL HANDLE

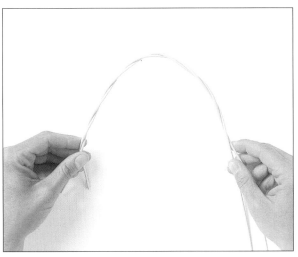

This handle is suitable for small baskets, including those to be hung on the wall.
Take a weaving rod and dampen it. Bend it in half and wrap the two parts round each other.

Now thread this twisted handle into the border of a basket, plait the two parts to create a small arch, then fasten it externally.

RUSTIC HANDLE

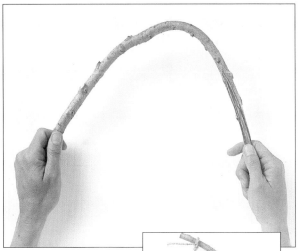

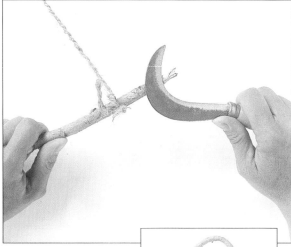

This rather rustic looking handle is made by bending a twig. Get a finger-sized one and if you wish you can strip it of its bark. Bend it and tie the ends with a string.

Leave it dry for a few weeks. Then sharpen the ends with a pruning hook and thread the handle in the sides.

TIPS

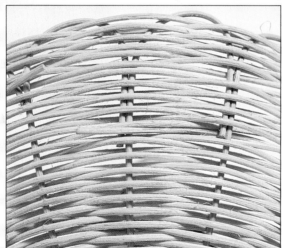

An old peasant who had been weaving all his life told me that a good basket could hold water. This means that when working a basket, plaiting and weaving must have the greatest possible number of rods and weaving rods. This way, there are no empty spaces. It is therefore very important to keep the weaving rods taut, using some force, to avoid use slackening the weaving. A well-made basket should last forever.

Be careful to hide the change of weaving rods by making oblique cuts to the tips, which protrude inside and outside the basket.
Remember that the size of the rods and of the weaving rods depends on the use of the basket. Use especially strong fibers particularly where the basket is very large, suitable for carrying considerable weights. And finally, do not forget to wet the fibers before working them.

FINISHING TOUCHES

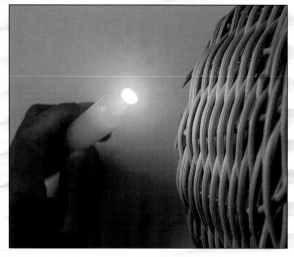

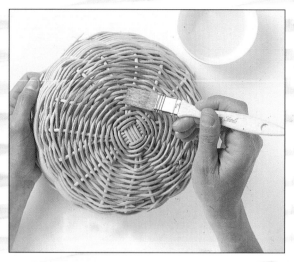

To eliminate the straw blades of the fiber, pass quickly and carefully the flame of a candle on both the inside and the outside surface of the basket.

Protect your work from humidity by giving it a very slight coat of glue or linseed oil.

REPAIRING A BASKET

Only when you have finished weaving your first basket will you be able to understand it's worth and how much care and work it cost you.

Therefore, if you come across an old basket, a bit damaged or even with broken rods, think twice before throwing it away and try and understand if it can be repaired. This is not an easy task because the basket must be handled with care to avoid breaking the fibers.

Wet the fibers, which are to be woven. Cut rods equal in size to those, which are broken. Sharpen the ends with the punch. Insert them beside the broken ones in the lower border. Repeat for the top border.

With two long weaving rods, fill in the empty space with two-element weaving. Color the fiber used for repairing the basket if it is not the same as the original.

SHAPES

BASKET WITH MANDLE

SIZE
6 13/16" (17 CM) - BASE DIAMETER
7 7/8" (20 CM) - DIAMETER TOP BORDER
12" (30 CM) - HEIGHT OF SIDES

MATERIALS
- 10 RODS (2/16") 36" (90 CM) LONG
- WEAVING RODS (1/16", 3/32", 2/16")
- VINYL GLUE
- SHEARS, CUTTER
- WEIGHTS
- PEGS
- PUNCH, METAL BAR
- VAPORIZER, FRUNING HOOK

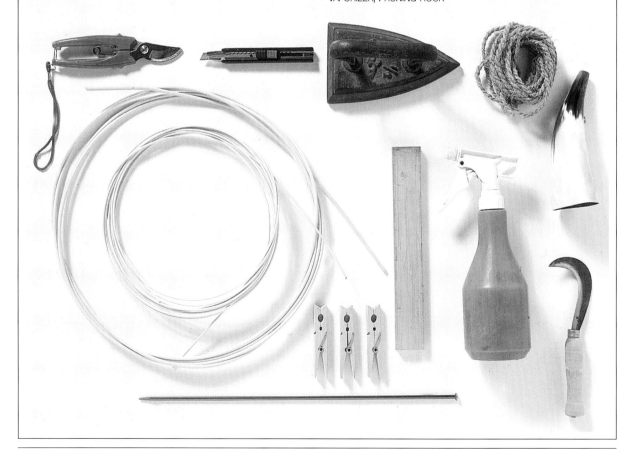

Position eight rods so as to make a circular base. With a slender bent weaving rod begin weaving with the over-under technique.
When the weaving rods are finished, proceed with another two of greater size. The circular base is finished when it reaches a diameter of about 6 13/16" (17 cm).

Now turn the work over and wet the rods well. Keep the base steady with a weight, take a cutter and make a slight cut in the part of the rod turned inwards.

Wet the rods well and bend them upwards. Tie them together at the top with a string.

The lower border is made by weaving three weaving rods for about three rounds. Proceed with two weaving rods as far as the upper edge.

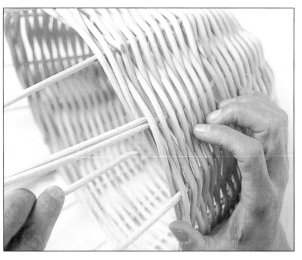

To make the handle, insert two rods of about 2/16" (4 mm) wide and 36" (90 cm) long along two opposite weaving rods in the sides.

Weave three more elements in the last upper part of the sides so as to make the basket stronger. Work the border with the end part of the rods, wetting them before bending them at 90°. This type of basket requires a robust border. Having finished the border, you can now make the handle, which also must be robust. Finish off the basket by clipping all the tips of the weaving rods, which protrude from the weaving. To make the basket even more solid, you could brush it with a coat of vinyl glue.

COLORED TRAY

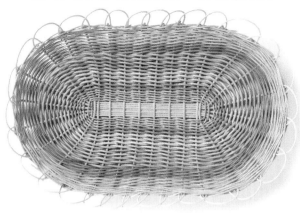

SIZE
BASE: 12" x 18" (30 x 45 CM)

MATERIALS
- 15 RODS 3/32" INCHES (3 MM) 20" (50 CM) LONG
- 3 1/16" (2 MM) WEAVING RODS FOR EACH COLOR
- SOME EQUAL SIZED WEAVING RODS IN A NATURAL COLOR
- NATURAL COLORS
- PUNCH, PEGS
- SHEARS, CUTTER
- PENCIL, PAINTBRUSH
- WATER PROOF TRANSPARENT PAINT
- VAPORIZER

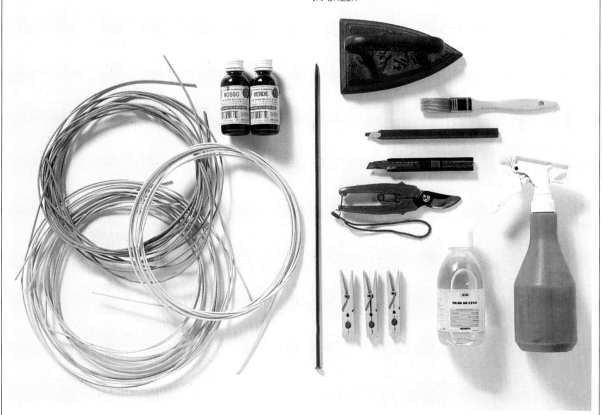

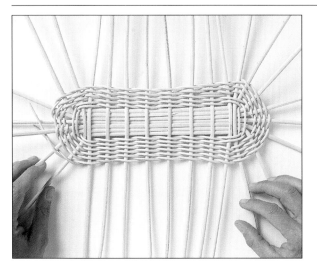

Place the rods as indicated for making an oval base. With a natural colored weaving rod bent in half, begin weaving with the under-over technique.

Weave four rounds and then change color, endeavoring to hide the point of changing the weaving rod in the lower part of the tray.

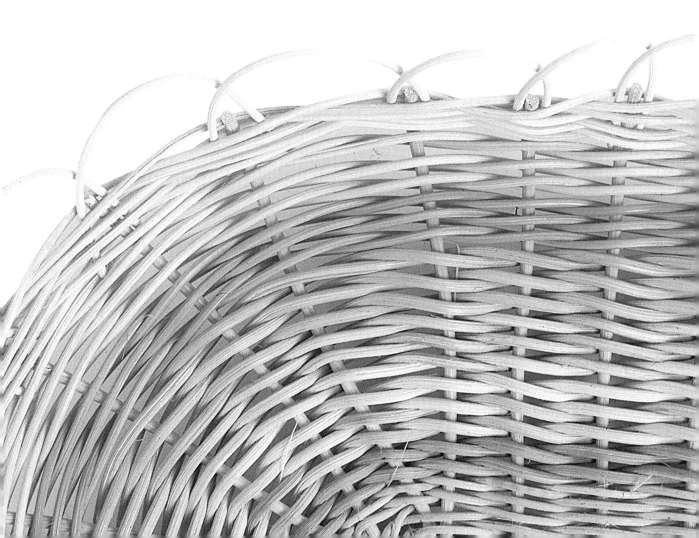

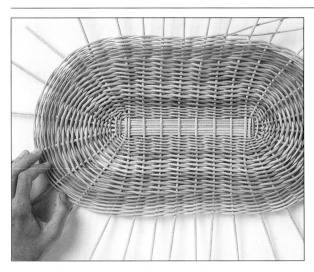

Proceed for two rounds with pink and then for six rounds with green. Alternate other colors and finish with three rounds of natural color.

Bend the rods upwards and weave three rounds of the sides. For the border, cut the rods which protrude from the side weaving and insert thinner rods, with which you can weave the simple type border. As the structure of this base tends to lose its shape, we recommend you wet it and press it with a weight of some kg for a whole night. Having put the finishing touches to the work, you can pass a coat of transparent water repellent paint to avoid damaging the tray through use.

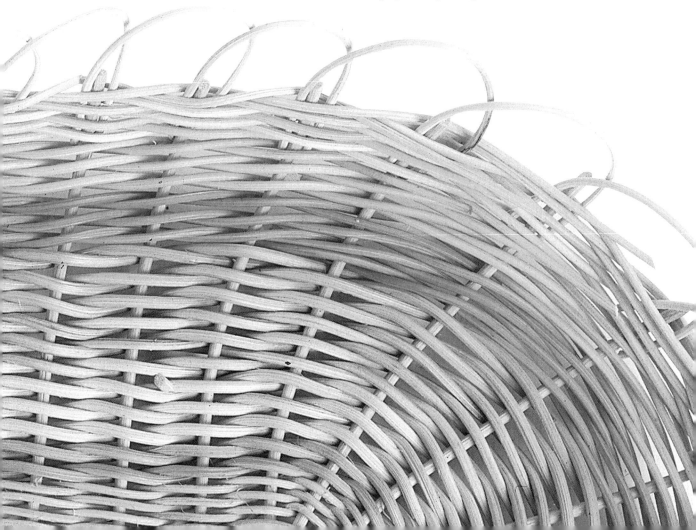

CONE-SHAPED BASKET

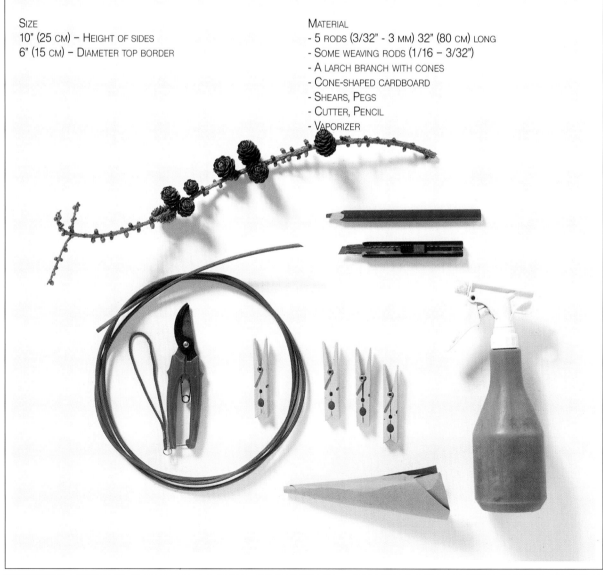

SIZE
10" (25 CM) – HEIGHT OF SIDES
6" (15 CM) – DIAMETER TOP BORDER

MATERIAL
- 5 RODS (3/32" - 3 MM) 32" (80 CM) LONG
- SOME WEAVING RODS (1/16 – 3/32")
- A LARCH BRANCH WITH CONES
- CONE-SHAPED CARDBOARD
- SHEARS, PEGS
- CUTTER, PENCIL
- VAPORIZER

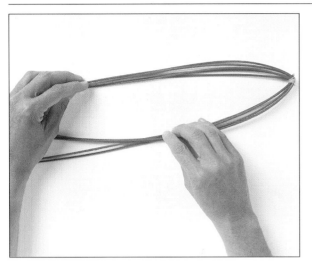

Take the five rods, bend them in half and fasten the fold by tying them with some thread.

Now position them so as to form a cone whose top corresponds to the binding. Pair the rods off two by two.

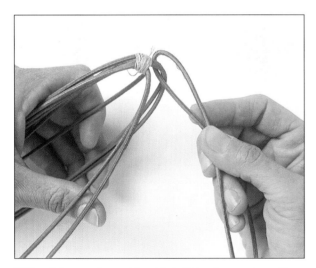

With a thin weaving rod bent in half, begin weaving with the over-under technique.

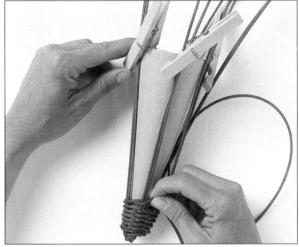

It may be useful to make a cone-shaped carbon support to slip in to the inner part and secure with some pegs to the rods.

Proceed to the end of the weaving rod, after which continue with another two of greater size. After about ten rounds, separate the rods and continue weaving keeping them well apart from each other. As you work, make sure the shape of the basket is the one desired.

When the work is finished, and before weaving the border, pass a thin branch of larch under-over leaving the pine cones to the outside of the basket. A type of small handle can be made on the top border to hang the basket on the wall.

OPEN-FRONT WALL BASKETS

SIZE
9 3/16" (23 CM) – BASE DIAMETER
6" (15 CM) – DEPTH

MATERIAL
- 6 RODS (2/16") 32" (80 CM) LONG
- WEAVING RODS (3/32 – 2/16")
- TAILOR'S MEASURING TAPE
- PENCIL, CUTTER
- PEGS, VAPORIZER
- SHEARS, ROPES

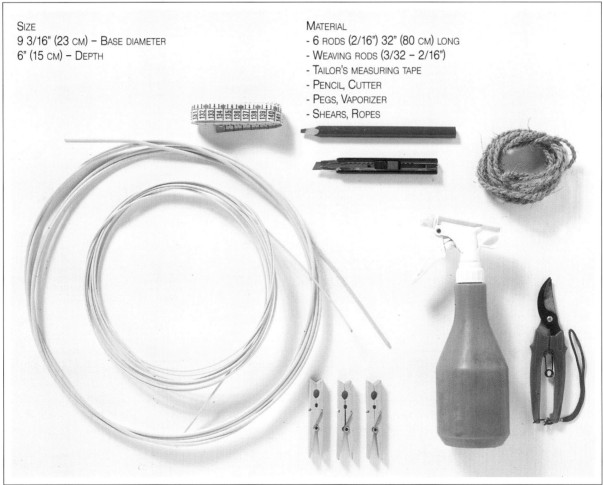

Place six rods crossways to make the circular base. You can follow the instructions given in the relative paragraph, but with a variation. Instead of making the cut coincide with the middle of the rod, cut it at a third. In this way, you have a Latin cross.

With a smaller weaving rod bent in half, weave eight or nine rounds for the base. Then use two bigger ones until the proposed diameter of about 9 3/16" (23 cm) is reached.

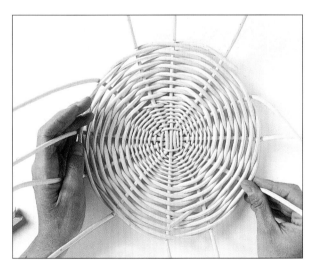

Turn the base over and bend the rods upwards. Bind the longest rods together with a string: in this way, the three shortest are excluded.

Weave three rounds of the side with two weaving rods of 2/16" (4 mm).

Then bend the three shorter rods at 90° and work the border.

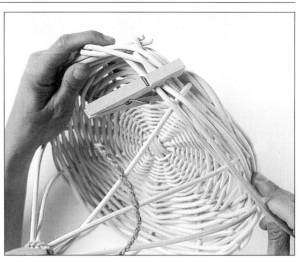

Proceed on the opposite side, weaving the weaving rods from one side to the other and interrupting the work every round. Always secure the ends inside the work.

Continue until the basket has reached the size and shape desired. Bend the remaining rods and work the border.

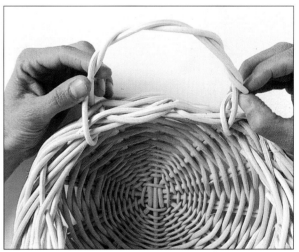

Fasten on a small handle and finish off the work.

RIBBED HANGING BASKET

Size: 7 3/16 x 10 6/16" (18 cm x 26 cm)
Length of handle 52" (130 cm)

Material
- Branch with 5 3/16" (13 cm) diameter
- 6 2/16" (4 mm) wide rods, of which one measuring 34" (85 cm) long and 5 16" (40 cm) long
- Weaving rods (3/32 – 2/16")
- Pruning hook, Cutter
- Paintbrush, Linseed oil
- Strong thread, Vaporizer
- Pegs
- Shears

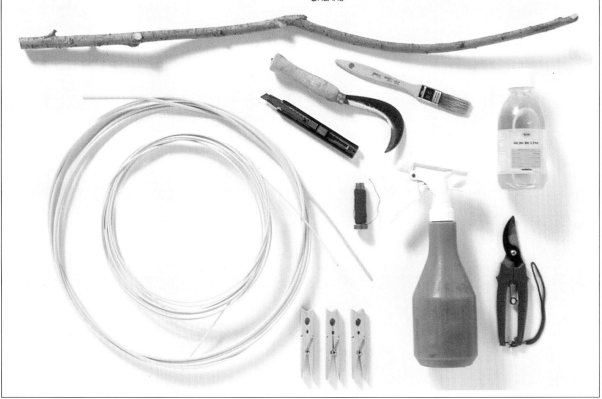

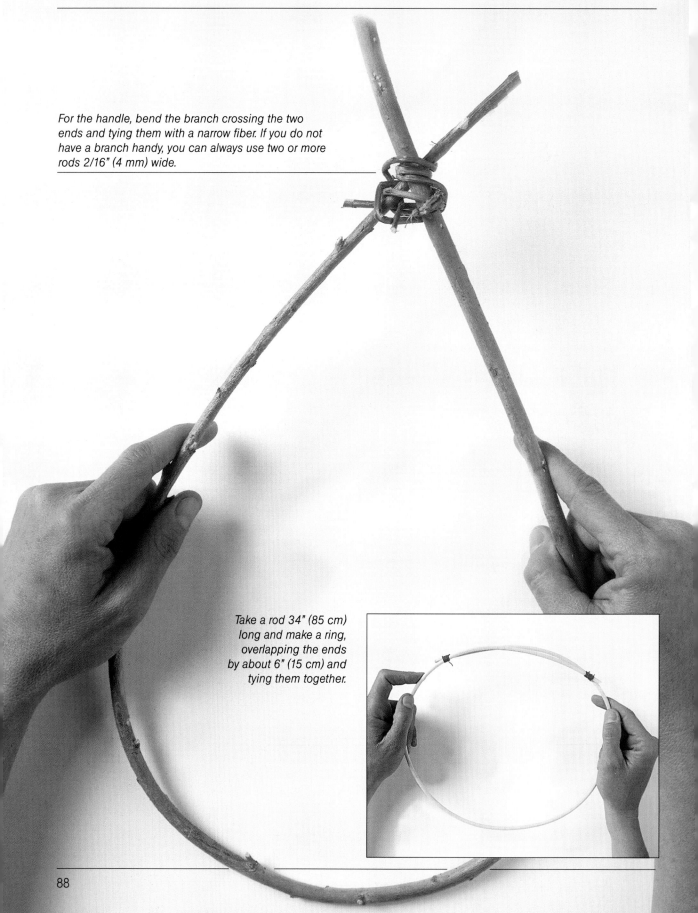

For the handle, bend the branch crossing the two ends and tying them with a narrow fiber. If you do not have a branch handy, you can always use two or more rods 2/16" (4 mm) wide.

Take a rod 34" (85 cm) long and make a ring, overlapping the ends by about 6" (15 cm) and tying them together.

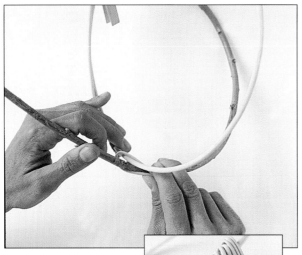

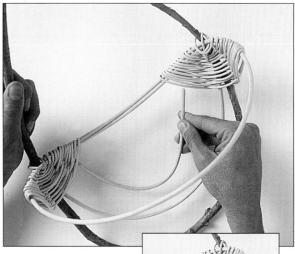

Secure the ring to the handle with a side fastening. To do this, use a weaving rod 3/32" (3 mm) wide. Three-element binding is made by weaving a fiber over-under the handle and the two parts of the ring which intersect with it. Keep the fiber taut.

Take five rods 16" (40 cm) long, sharpen their ends, and wet them. Then, insert them into the pockets that have formed in the side fastenings of the frame: the ribs will take on a semi-circle form, two of them will make up the back frame and the remaining three the front one.

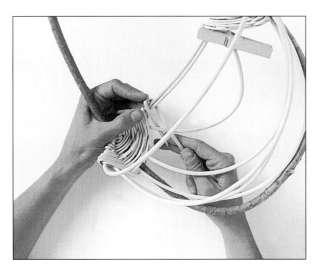

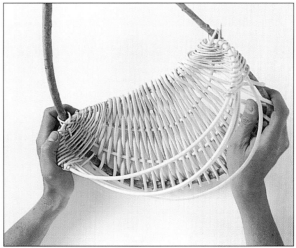

To keep the weaving straight it is important to keep the same distance between one rib and the other both in the front and the back part.
Take a weaving rod 2/16" (4 mm) and start weaving the back part, passing over-under the ribs and around the rods of the frame.

Once you have completed the back part, repeat the same procedure for the front part, trying to maintain the rounded convex shape. When you change the weaving rod, insert the end towards the inside of the basket.
To finish, clip the protruding parts obliquely and give the basket a coat of linseed oil.

WREATHS

If you wish to make wreaths
emanating perfumed
essences, such as lavender
or rosemary twist a bunch
of branches and tie it with a
slender twig. Decorated
with ribbons and flowers,
this wreath can be used to
perfume rooms pleasantly.

SIZE
10 3/16" (27 CM) DIAMETER

MATERIAL
- RODS (2/16" - 4 MM)
- SHEARS
- PEGS
- VAPORIZER

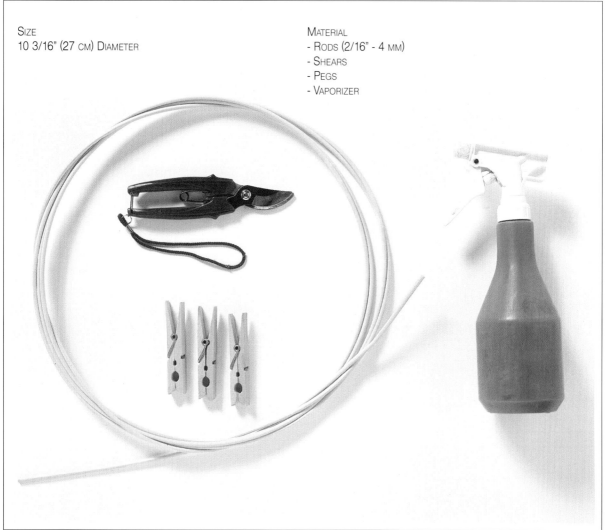

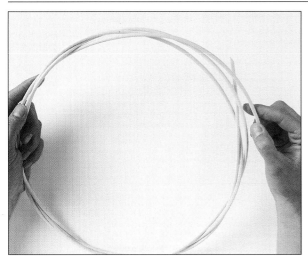

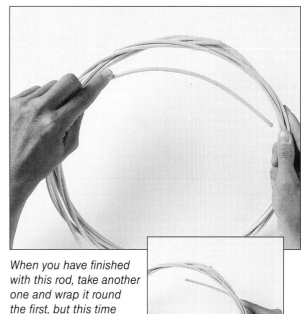

Take a rod and bend it, making a circle of the width desired. Then, with one end, twist around this, passing clockwise from the inside to the outside of the circle.

When you have finished with this rod, take another one and wrap it round the first, but this time anti-clockwise. Proceed in this way until you have reached the size desired.

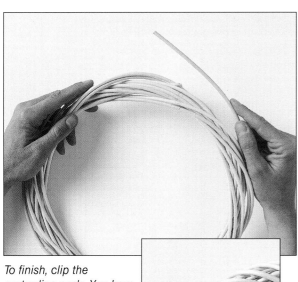

To finish, clip the protruding ends. You have now made a wreath.

PLAIT

SIZE: 20" (50 CM)

MATERIAL
- A SKEIN OF RAFFIA OR STRAW 24" (60 CM) LONG
- RED CLOTH RIBBON
- PEGS
- CUTTER, SHEARS

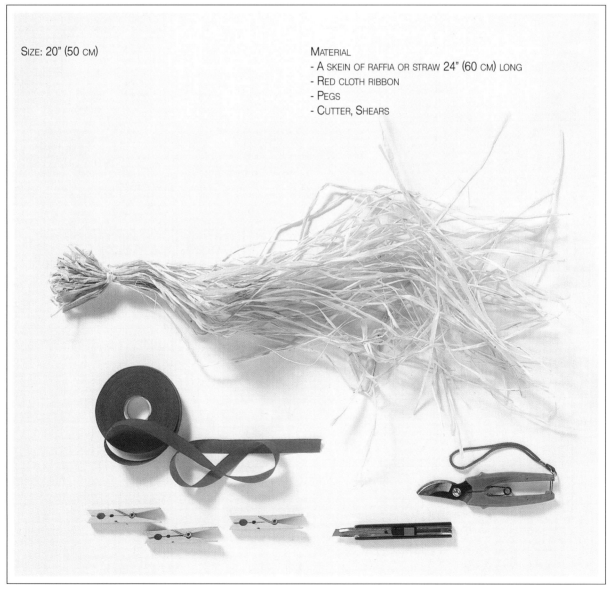

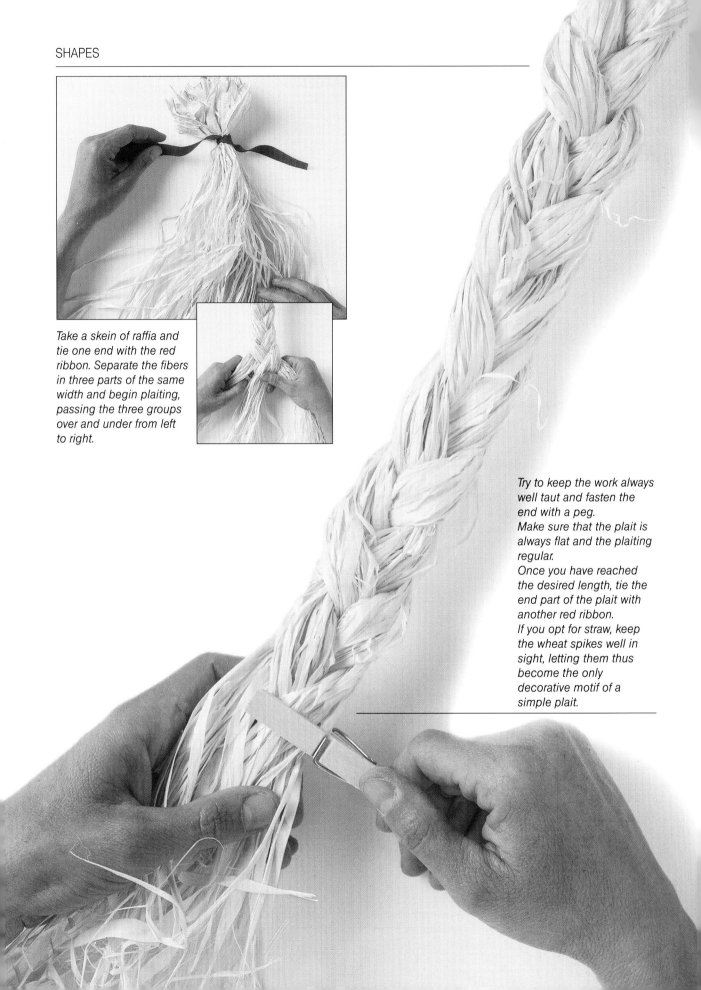

Take a skein of raffia and tie one end with the red ribbon. Separate the fibers in three parts of the same width and begin plaiting, passing the three groups over and under from left to right.

Try to keep the work always well taut and fasten the end with a peg.
Make sure that the plait is always flat and the plaiting regular.
Once you have reached the desired length, tie the end part of the plait with another red ribbon.
If you opt for straw, keep the wheat spikes well in sight, letting them thus become the only decorative motif of a simple plait.

FESTOON

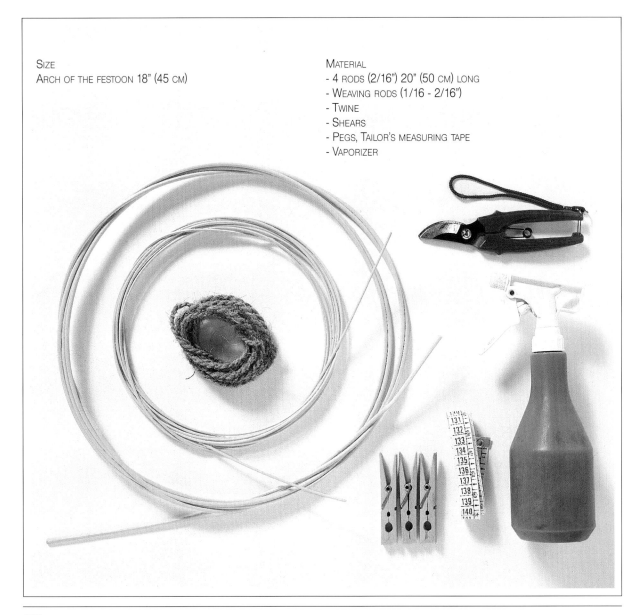

SIZE
ARCH OF THE FESTOON 18" (45 CM)

MATERIAL
- 4 RODS (2/16") 20" (50 CM) LONG
- WEAVING RODS (1/16 - 2/16")
- TWINE
- SHEARS
- PEGS, TAILOR'S MEASURING TAPE
- VAPORIZER

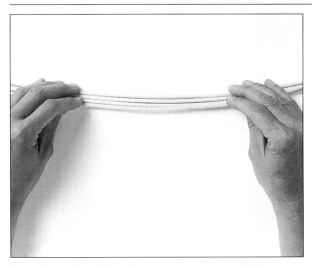

Take four rods and wet them to ease your work. Place them alongside one another.

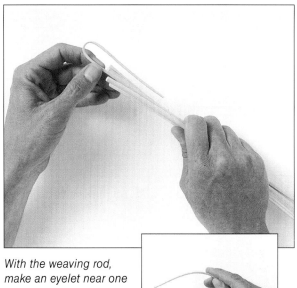

With the weaving rod, make an eyelet near one end of the rods and pass them over the whole length until the other end, where you will bend the fiber to make another eyelet.

Secure the rods through tight twisting and wet them well. Now bend them arch-like and tie the two ends with some twine.

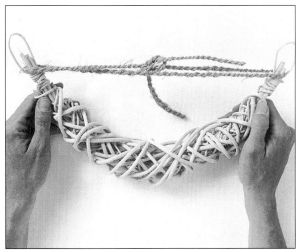

Take a weaving rod and wrap it round the rods from left to right and vice-versa, trying to create greater thickness at the center of the festoon. When you have completed your work, clip the ends and leave the festoon to dry before untying it. Your festoon is now ready to be decorated.

WEAVING
SUGGESTIONS

TRAY

Here are many multi-functional, easy-to-make trays,
worked with the technique indicated for making a circular base.

These two circular bases are of the same structure but are made with different materials: one is made with medulla, very regular and rather a refined piece of work. The other, made with wood essences, is more irregular and rustic.

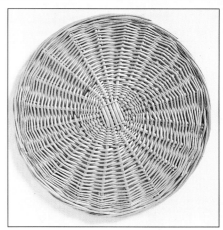

The frame of this model is made up of a circular base and two arches. The weaving rods are all parallel and woven over-under the rods. Two small handles give a finishing touch to the tray.

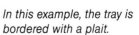

In this example, the tray is bordered with a plait.

This large centerpiece was carefully woven with wicker fibers, following the technique used for circular bases.

These fruit baskets were made with a circular base and woven with colored fibers ending with a simple plait on the border.

These trays, used for drying fresh pasta, were made following the oval base technique. The side weaving, which is very low, ends with a plaited border.

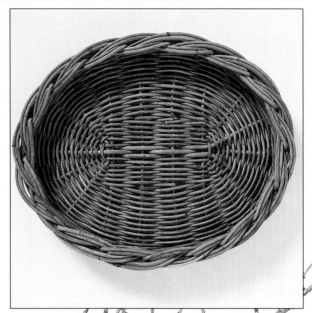

BASKETS, HAMPERS

A lemon basket made with fibers taken from the weeping willow is depicted on this page.
It has a circular base and its sides are slightly flared.

This circular-based basket was made with wood fibers and has a slender handle made from a branch stripped of its bark.

This basket is also circular-based but its long, arch-like handle is plaited and fastened to the sides..

This basket, made with wood essences, has a very simple oval base and a plaited handle and border.

Two robust, oval-based baskets made with unprocessed fibers and woven according to the oldest peasant traditions are Depicted on these pages. The handles are made of branches stripped of their bark.

The handle of this oval-based basket forms a wide arch.
The weaving, with the warp and woof of different fibers in
the sides, ends with a plaited border.

The base of this rustic basket made of fibers taken from the weeping willow develops lengthwise. Its woven sides give it a low level shape, particularly harmonious along the shorter sides.

The base is certainly most original part of these objects. In the two baskets with the arch-like handles the color changes with regard to the rest of the work. In the basket with the two small handles, the large strips of the rods are interlaced and left wide-meshed.

The rods of this circular-based basket were fastened to a walking stick. It makes an unusual decorative object for your country house and will come in handy when out picking mushrooms or wild fruits.

*This cone-shaped basket
was made with vine shoots.*

This rectangular-shaped shopping basket has two flexible handles fastened to the border with small metal rings.

The traditional big breadbasket depicted on this page was made with fibers from the weeping willow. It has a rectangular base and two robust, comfortable handles, which pick up the motif weaving along the border.

This oval-based basket was made with purple-dyed fibers and was woven with two weaving rods following the over-under technique. Its handle make it possible to carry it on one's arm.

Oblique weaving along the sides characterize this circular-shaped work basket. The weaving of the border is picked up as a decorative motif on the sides.

HANGING BASKETS

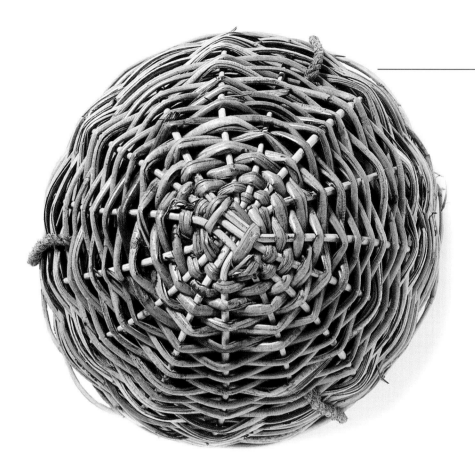

This is a typical semi-circular basket, which can be fastened to the ceiling with a strong rope. It is simple to make: one starts from a circular base and goes on to modeling a concave shape.

Two large branches stripped of their bark, one straight and the other bent arch-wise, shape this wall vase-holder. Its pattern is typical rib weaving. It can be hung on the wall with a large piece of untreated rope fastened to the ends of the horizontal rod.

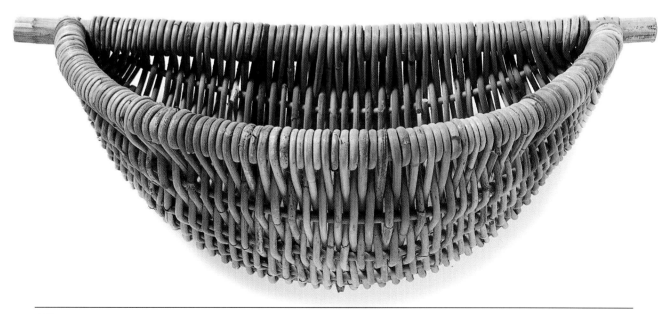

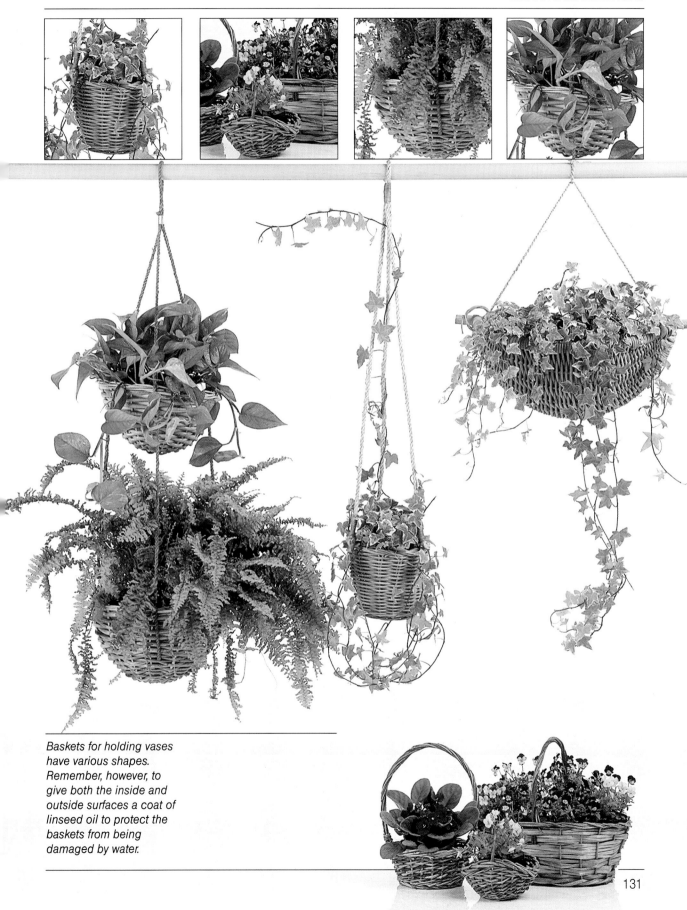

Baskets for holding vases have various shapes. Remember, however, to give both the inside and outside surfaces a coat of linseed oil to protect the baskets from being damaged by water.

131

LARGE BASKETS FOR THE HOUSE

This classical oval-based laundry basket was woven with thick fibers. It has a very large border and two small side openings for being carried.

From a circular base, with strong rods, it is possible to weave a large cylindrical container to put in the garden for use as a rubbish basket. The lid is fastened with a weaving rod to the back part and at the sides there are two small handles with which to lift it.

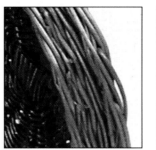
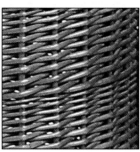

The corners of this rectangular-shaped wicker trunk were strengthened with very large rods, or ribs, making up the frame.
A small plait with an eyelet serves to close the lid.

This is a lovely, extremely useful basket, with its front part lower than the back. It has a small handle fixed on one side to help move it about.

The sides of this oval-based wicker dog basket are woven with rods bent at 90°. The front part of the basket is lower to give the dog an entrance. Clip the inside of the basket very well, making sure you have got rid of all the dangerous protruding parts.

This large trunk made with medulla dyed in dark green in which to store your children's toys requires a lot of work but no particular skill. The frame is made with robust ribs along all the corners.

FURNISHINGS

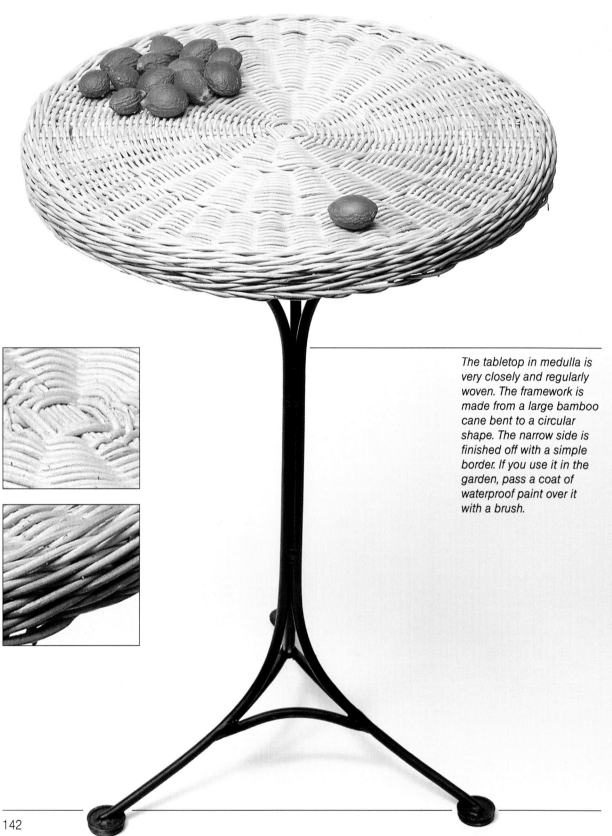

The tabletop in medulla is very closely and regularly woven. The framework is made from a large bamboo cane bent to a circular shape. The narrow side is finished off with a simple border. If you use it in the garden, pass a coat of waterproof paint over it with a brush.

To make this shade, begin weaving from the metal structure of the lamp. The ribs are fastened to the circles of the two bases and work is done with the weaving rods only on the side, using the over-under technique and being careful to keep the desired shape all along.

ORDER IN THE KITCHEN

These small baskets for holding cutlery will add a warm note to your kitchen. The structure is in wood while the drawers are small baskets with a rectangular base and two windows, which act as handles.

A small bottle-holding stand in an absolutely natural style is here created with separate cylindrical elements joined together through the very tight binding of the upper borders.

SETTING THE TABLE WITH MEDULLA

Natural fiber goes extremely well with the white china set out on this table. The shapes are simple and the weaving very regular. The small plaits of the handles and the borders create a decorative element.

*White medulla is used for this small round container
A final coat of linseed oil will protect it from temperature
changes, while a coat given every now and again will
preserve it in time.*

...AND WITH RUSTIC WICKER

Your table will take on another look if you use rustic wicker instead of delicate medulla to hold glasses and bottles. If you wet the wicker in summer the drinks will stay fresher longer. You can also use wicker to transform your dishes and so complete your table set.

WITH WHEELS

A shopping basket must certainly have a strong base, so use rods of greater size than the weaving rods and keep the weaving very close. This is so for the sides as well, and you will find a metal bar indispensable for keeping the weave close. The lid is fitted to the back and the handle is inserted in the side weaving from the base on. The board with the wheels is fixed just above the base.

The hood of this attractive pram for dolls is decorated with a fretwork and finished off with a plait. The handle is robust and the wheels are fixed to a wooden frame.

WREATHS

A rustic wreath with openwork weaving to create a simple frame, and decorated wreaths which turn into an attractive Christmas centerpiece with candles, or into a festive decoration for hanging up.

LEISURE TIME

Before beginning a bicycle basket carefully measure the handlebars and the space between them and the front wheel. You now have the exact dimensions for an oval base basket. A folding handle will make it more practical. Remember to leave an opening for the lamp and, when finished, brush on a coat of waterproof paint.

Two-tone wicker is used for this picnic hamper. The base is square and small dividing panels separate the glasses from the other dishes. The handles and leather straps are fastened outside to the front side.

Here are two containers in natural fibers designed for sport: colored medulla is advised for the fisherman's basket and strong wicker for the golf-bag. Both have a hemp shoulder strap.

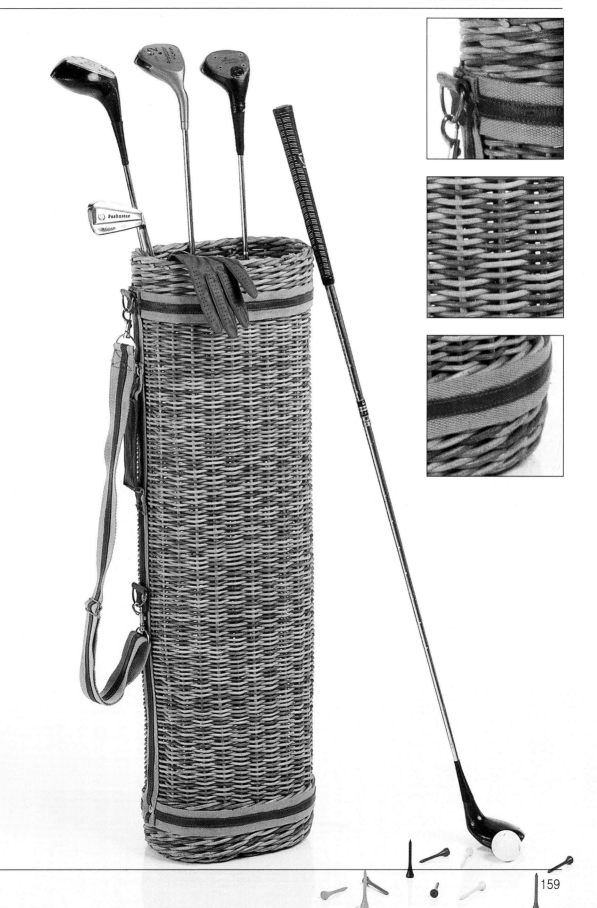

GLOSSARY

Clipping: a phase of the work in which the protruding tips of the weaving rods are clipped off with a sharp shears. The cut is made obliquely.

Dyeing: technique for coloring the fibers used in weaving.

Fastening: a phase in the work in which a part of the basket is fixed to another. These can have two or more elements and various types of junctures.

Frame: a bearing structure suitable for supporting certain types of basket. Normally it is made up of fibers, which are bigger with respect to the work.

Handle: this part of the basket, which may have various shapes, can also constitute an element of the frame structure.

Ribs: Rods making up the frame of a basket.

Rods: fibers of greater width, which form the base structure, and then, bent at 90°, continue along the sides.

Sharpen: Reduce the width of a rod, usually with a pruning hook so as to be able to insert it in the weaving.

Strips: narrow bands of fiber, which make up the warp or the woof of the weaving.

Warp: A group of fibers used to form the length of the woven piece, normally carried out with wider fibers placed parallel alongside.

Weaving: A technique in which the woof and the warp are made up by fibers of different width, greater for the former and lesser for the latter.

Weaving rod: a narrower fiber, which is used to interweave. It creates the woof in weaving.

Woof: a group of fibers placed parallel to each other which cross the warp and make up the texture.

INDEX